SADDAM

THE FACE OF EVIL

...inside the
horrific mind
of the Butcher
of Baghdad...

BY MARK CANTRELL AND RONALD VAUGHAN

Edited by Nicholas Maier

AMI BOOKS

American Media Inc.

SADDAM
The Face of Evil

Copyright © 2003 AMI Books, Inc.

Cover design: Carlos Plaza
Interior design: Debbie Browning

ISBN: 1-932270-20-5

First printing: June 2003

Printed in the United States of America

10 9 8 7 6 5 4 3 2 1

DEDICATION

The authors wish to dedicate this book to the brave American and coalition forces who fought valiantly to defeat Saddam Hussein, especially those who selflessly gave their lives during Operation Iraqi Freedom.

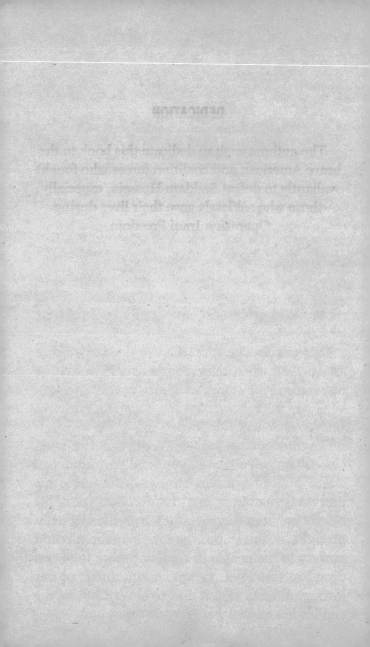

INTRODUCTION

EVIL INCARNATE

What kind of ruler murders his own subjects with poison gas?

That was the question the world was forced to ask in 1988 when television images revealed the massacre of thousands of Kurds in northern Iraq — entire villages put to death on the whim of Iraqi President Saddam Hussein.

The Middle East has been torn by violence and bloodshed for centuries, but Saddam introduced a new level of brutality to the region. From his first assassination at age 15 to the final fall of his bloody regime, the dictator's iron-fisted tactics brought nothing but terror, heartbreak and poverty to the people of Iraq. For more than two decades this evil tyrant maintained power through threats, deceit and treachery, but in the end his lies and trickery couldn't save him.

When coalition forces finally brought down Saddam's empire, they found that the Butcher of Baghdad had denied himself no luxury, living in opulent splendor while his subjects scrambled for basic necessities. His palaces were lined with priceless paintings, gilded with gems and precious metals and boasted gold-plated plumbing. The nation's liberators even uncovered a hidden love nest where Saddam and his mistress often rendezvoused. The retreat, decked out in garish '60s-era decor, featured a king-size bed flanked by mirrors, a whirlpool bath and paintings of topless women. When served meals there, Saddam and his concubine dined on the stolen dinnerware of the Kuwaiti royal family, who he briefly drove into exile during his power-mad 1990 invasion of that tiny country.

But Saddam's love of excess didn't just limit itself to amenities. When it came to getting what he wanted and crushing his enemies, his ruthlessness was truly without equal. After the liberation of Baghdad, coalition troops discovered underground detention centers where Saddam's henchmen systematically tortured prisoners, using the most heinous methods imaginable to extract information or simply indulge their passion for human suffering.

In one such prison, soldiers found death chambers with rusted shackles on the bare walls and floors caked with dried blood. Bookshelves in the facility were filled with photo albums of Saddam's victims, their eyes gouged out, genitals charred and throats slashed.

Such inhumanity was the rule rather than the exception in Saddam's world, where even a hint of disagreement was grounds for execution. His complete disregard for human life has assured him a place among history's most evil despots — and his two wicked sons have also earned their place beside him in hell.

It's hard to imagine how an entity of such pure evil could rise to power in our supposedly modern world. We can only pray that such horrific crimes against humanity never happen again.

CHAPTER ONE

METHODS OF MADNESS

The two terrified men are dragged into the schoolyard, kicking and screaming. As 200 invited observers look on, the men are shoved onto the muddy ground and their heads forced onto a low brick wall. As the two struggle against their captors, members of Saddam Hussein's Fedayeen Saddam, a ruthless paramilitary gang led by his son, step forward. They force the men's mouths open and tear out their tongues with pliers, then step back as an executioner delivers merciful death, beheading them with the blade of a scimitar. To one side, a cameraman records the grisly scene for Saddam's later enjoyment.

Until recently, these were the facts of life — and death — in Saddam's world, where dissension was forbidden, punishable by torture and worse. Mere suspicion was enough to spell doom for the bloody tyrant's own people; in this case, the victims were suspected of aiding opposition forces in the south of Iraq. In Saddamland, no one dared even whisper a hint of disagreement with government policy, for fear of finding themselves in one of the evil dictator's infamous torture chambers, knowing that both they and their families would inevitably face agonizing pain and certain death. In a country where Saddam's power was absolute, his relatives and favored henchmen were free to do as they pleased, whether it was murder, kidnapping, extortion or rape.

To suppress any kind of disloyalty, Saddam ruled Iraq with the politics of terror from the moment he took power in 1979. At that time Iraq was a flourishing nation, its coffers overflowing with a $37 million surplus, but Saddam quickly ended the nation's economic prosperity. In less than a quarter-century he managed to drive the once-proud nation into grinding poverty, rendering most of his subjects completely dependent on his corrupt government for such basic necessities as food and medicine. Although he often boasted of his subjects' loyalty, Saddam brought nothing to his country but misery and grief. Since his rise to power, Iraq has seen only a scant three years where it was not involved in a war or burdened by international economic sanctions.

Yet Saddam always had an easy explanation

for Iraq's hardships: It's the fault of the West, particularly the United States, he claimed, even as he gilded his palaces with gold and enjoyed a privileged life of comfort while his subjects lived in filth. He was even known to possess a gold-plated carriage. In a desert country where water is a precious commodity, every one of his palaces featured a large pool and many had fountains, indoor streams and even waterfalls. A true megalomaniac, Saddam wallpapered Iraq with huge posters and paintings of himself, always in some heroic pose. But there was nothing heroic about the wholesale slaughter of thousands of his subjects, a scenario that was carried out countless times during his brutal regime.

What is known about Saddam's private life might lead anyone to conclude that he was a madman. When the woman who had been Saddam's consort for more then 30 years was interviewed, she revealed that he actually boasted about his attempt to kill his son Uday, a bloodthirsty monster in his own right.

Those who requested a meeting with the dictator were usually kept waiting for weeks, with no guarantee of seeing Saddam. Foreign dignitaries were routinely dumped at guesthouses where they languished, wondering when — or if — they'd be granted an audience.

While most of his countrymen lived in abject

poverty, Saddam enjoyed some of the finest cuisine in the world: Lobster, shrimp and fish, choice cuts of meat and plenty of fresh dairy products were flown in fresh twice a week. Before it came near him, however, the food was sent to his nuclear scientists, X-rayed and tested for poison or radioactive contamination.

Moreover, when it came to hygiene, Saddam seemed to subscribe to the Howard Hughes school: He insisted that visitors' hands be washed in as many as three different disinfectants before they were allowed into the same room with him and that their clothing be washed, sterilized and X-rayed as well. When the dictator did allow visitors, he demanded they greet him with a ceremonial armpit kiss.

Ironically, he regularly advised his subjects on matters of personal hygiene. In the film *Uncle Saddam*, a documentary lensed by French film maker Joel Soler, the dictator is shown behind a desk wearing a Western-style suit and a hat with a wide brim, holding forth on body odor: "It's not appropriate for someone to attend a gathering or to be with his children with his body odor trailing behind emitting a sweet or stinky smell mixed with perspiration. It's preferable to bathe twice a day, but at least once a day. And when the male bathes once a day, the female should bathe twice a day, (the) female is more delicate, and the smell

of a woman is more noticeable than the male."
The film also notes that Saddam retained a team
of doctors to adjust the temperature of his office
just so, that he loved to fire rifles into the air at
social occasions and that his idea of sport fishing
was tossing hand grenades into a pond.

Demonstrating how far Saddam's reach truly
extended, when Soler returned to the United
States after filming the documentary he found
his home splashed with red paint and his garbage
cans filled with gasoline and ignited. The perpe-
trator had left this note: "In the name of Allah,
the merciful and compassionate, burn this satanic
film or you will be dead."

With all his strange habits, it's tempting to
dismiss Saddam as merely crazy. But most psychi-
atrists agree that the truth is much more complex
than that — there was usually some method to his
madness. Experts say the careful attention to his
visitors was designed to prevent someone from
sneaking in a weapon or biological agent. Keeping
visitors waiting was a power tactic to let prospec-
tive guests know from the outset exactly who was
in control. Even Saddam's fascination with
firearms might have been a warning to his rivals.

During an interview, Joe Wilson, former
ambassador to Kuwait, recalled meeting Saddam
four days after the Iraqi invasion of that country
in 1991. He remembered that looking into

Saddam's eyes was like staring into the gaze of a cobra. "Somebody once told me that the look he gave his visitors was reptilian, like a snake hypnotizing its prey. And that's clearly what he was trying to do ... create an atmosphere where he was in charge and where I was to be the intimidated one."

Wilson reported that one of Saddam's tactics of intimidation was to immediately invade a visitor's space, positioning himself a few inches away and then fixing the guest with his cold, unblinking stare. "When the time comes to shake hands, he puts his hand low," Wilson said. "And the minute you go for his hand, you're caught on camera bowing to the potentate."

But for a man possessing absolute power in his own country, Saddam often seemed fearful and paranoid. He created identical rooms in each of his more than 20 palaces where he conducted video appearances, making it impossible for potential assassins to pinpoint his location. He had a team of surgically enhanced look-alikes that could be called upon to perform his official duties, especially when those functions might have exposed him to danger. In 1990, Saddam even dispatched one of his look-alikes to meet Egyptian President Hosni Mubarak at the Baghdad airport.

Iraqi defectors have reported that Saddam slept

only two or three hours a night and was always armed. He had meals prepared for himself at several locations around Iraq, so that no one would know exactly which meal he would actually consume. At all the other locations, his staff was required to complete an elaborate serving ritual as if he was actually there. He built extensive and ornate bunkers beneath his palaces and decked them out with all the latest technological communications gear. And in most cases, Saddam reportedly didn't even consult with his closest aides when planning major moves.

Clearly, Saddam was a man on the run. Every night he moved under the cover of darkness from one location to another, accompanied by a security team of around 3,600 armed guards, anti-aircraft and anti-tank battalions and even a field hospital. And, for an extra measure of mobility, he outfitted three large trucks with living quarters. All his precautions were for good reason — there had been four attempts on his life since 1990, some of them mounted by members of his own Republican Guard and Special Republican Guard, the very units said to be most loyal to him. And yet Saddam still claimed to be loved by the Iraqi people.

Rather than finding him insane, one psychiatrist diagnosed Saddam's mental state as "malignant narcissism," meaning an inability to relate to others' suffering mixed with paranoia and a drive to use whatever means necessary to achieve his goals. Many analysts feel those goals included not only ruling the Arab world but orchestrating the elimination of Western civilization.

Saddam's bigoted ravings made it abundantly clear that his racism was in the tradition of Hitler, who believed that the Germans were a master race and all others — especially the Jews — were inferior and deserved to perish. Saddam viewed the West in the same way, but more than simply considering us inferior, he was convinced that Western influences were polluting the Arab world and diluting its purity. That's why Saddam would have liked nothing more than to see each man, woman and child in the United States suffer the kind of torture and murder he dealt Iraqi dissidents. He lived by the credo set down by the founder of his own Baath Party, which began its rise in the 1940s: "When we are cruel to others, we know that our cruelty is in order to bring them back to their true selves of which they are ignorant."

Despite these inhuman beliefs, Saddam painted himself as a religious man, building mosques and making sure that posters of him at prayer were scattered across Iraq. In a 2003 interview, professor Edmund Ghareeb, author of the book *War in the Gulf, 1990-'91*, described how Saddam became a wolf in sheep's clothing, wrapping himself in Islamic ideals while his murderous campaign continued unchecked: "Saddam Hussein ... has been moving toward the Islamic side in the sense that he has ... spent a lot of money trying to build the biggest mosque in the world. He's asked students and officers to memorize the Koran or parts of the Koran and he has tried to improve his ties with the religious establishment, partly because he comes from this secular background, and there are questions about his background by the Islamists."

Even if Saddam wasn't particularly religious or insane, he was certainly capable of gross self-delusion. Where most of the world saw the end of the Gulf War as a major defeat for Iraq, the dictator continued to view it as one of his finest moments. One reason for that was that after the dust had settled, he was still in power. President George Herbert Walker Bush had decided that pursuing the fleeing Iraqi army into Baghdad would make the United States seem cruel and, besides, the United Nations mandate for war had called for the liberation of Kuwait, not the ousting of Saddam. Still, a postwar Saddam saw the U.S. failure to press on as a great victory, claiming that American forces turned back because of the threat of his weapons of mass destruction.

In an interview, psychiatrist Jerrold Post explained how Saddam could turn such a crushing defeat into victory: "The West saw this as a remark-

able, decisive military defeat, (but) the Gulf crisis
for him was the actualization of his dreams of glory.
Shortly after the invasion of Kuwait, to his aston-
ishment, the Palestinians were shouting his praises
in Jordan, Gaza and the occupied territories. He
could give a guttural grunt and the price of oil per
barrel would jump and the Dow Jones average
would drop — he had the world by the throat,
he was a major world leader, internationally
recognized at last."

Dreams of such glory had filled Saddam's head
since he was a child, but no public figure inspired
him more or served as a greater role model than
Joseph Stalin, the bloodthirsty Russian dictator.
Saddam's devotion to his murderous idol was displayed in one of his palace libraries, where Stalin's
writings filled the entire room. Like Stalin, Saddam
was raised in poverty by a single parent and both
men used assassination, conspiracy and secret
police to establish and retain power. To understand
how Saddam came to be the embodiment of evil in
the 21st century, it's helpful to look back at the
cold-blooded killer he admired so much.

Like Saddam, Stalin grew up under the cruel
hand of an alcoholic father who beat him and in
his rise to power murdered anyone who stood in
his way. He took the name Stalin because it meant
"man of steel." As a member of the Bolshevik
Party Stalin was exiled — twice — from his coun-

try in the early 1900s; Saddam was banished from Iraq early in his career with the Baath Party.

With the Russian Revolution in 1917, Stalin was able to return from Siberia and begin his homicidal march to power. He was named General Secretary of Russia in 1922 and immediately set to work seizing as much power as he could in the Communist Party, which was then firmly in control of the country.

In 1924, Russia's leader Vladimir Lenin died, spurring Stalin, his archrival Leon Trotsky and other Communist Party officials into an intense, cutthroat power struggle. When the dust finally cleared in 1927, Stalin had emerged the victor and Trotsky found himself in exile. Unable to tolerate the thought of his old nemesis running free, Stalin eventually sent his secret service to track Trotsky down and kill him, which they did in Mexico City in 1940.

When Stalin became the supreme Soviet leader in 1928, he inherited a diverse country composed of numerous tribes and ethnic groups just as Saddam would later. Stalin immediately set to work modernizing the country in order to spur economic prosperity, but his plan came at the expense of millions of lives.

This was especially true in the Ukraine, where most villages had collective farms. With the rise of Communism, they were ordered to turn over a large percentage of their crops to the government and many resisted. Furious that mere peasants would dare defy him, Stalin raised the quota of grain that farmers were forced to turn over to the state, resulting in disastrous food shortages in the Ukraine. It's estimated that between 6 million and 7 million people starved to death between 1932 and 1933 as a direct result of Stalin's engineered famine. And that was only one of his atrocities. His so-called Five Year Plans to industrialize Russia employed male convicts forced into backbreaking labor and millions died in Stalin's gulags, literally worked to death.

As with Saddam, Stalin's paranoia was an overwhelming factor in many of his crimes. He was obsessed with weeding out anyone who disagreed with him to even the slightest degree and he consolidated his vast power using torture and murder, wiping out millions of party members and ordinary civilians suspected of disloyalty. Between purges and famine, it's estimated that nearly a third of Russia's young men eventually perished under Stalin's iron fist.

Stalin was especially distrustful of the country's wealthier peasants — known as *kulaks* — and targeted them in large numbers for death. In his book *Harvest of Sorrow*, Robert Conquest writes that "in Kiev jail they are reported at this time shooting 70-120 men a night" and tells of "the Ukrainian village of Velyki Solontsi where, after 52 men had been removed as *kulaks*, their women and children were taken, dumped on a sandy stretch along the Vorskla River and left there."

In 1934, Sergei Kirov, a prominent and popular Communist Party leader, was assassinated in Leningrad. Although the hit was reportedly engineered by Stalin himself, he quickly passed immediate "security" legislation that eliminated any kind of due process for suspects and allowed the dreaded NKVD, Stalin's secret police, to execute them without trial. Stalin further used Kirov's death to rain unprecedented horror on his rivals, torturing them and their families to extract "confessions" that spelled their instant doom. His agents swept through the Red Army, massacring or imprisoning more than 35,000 officers suspected of treason. As terror spread through Russia, ordinary citizens — in an effort to avoid being arrested on bogus charges — began to turn in their neighbors for suspected crimes against the government, leading to more mass arrests and more deaths. The wives of arrested men were also sent to prison, where they were raped by male inmates. Even members of Stalin's own Secret Service were not above suspicion. One NKVD officer who found himself under arrest observed that "blind chance rules a man's life in this country of ours."

By the end of the 1930s, one in 20 Russian citizens had been arrested; the jails and the grave-yards were full. Conquest estimates that from 1937 to 1938 alone, more than 7 million people were arrested by Stalin's regime, joining the millions already languishing in prison, and a million of those were executed. He calculates that by the end of 1938, more than 11 million had died in jails and prison camps. And it was Stalin's paranoid obsession, like Saddam's much later, that had reduced the country to a shambles. His lofty plans to industrialize Russia lay in ruins and when he died in 1953, his successor Nikita Khrushchev was left the daunting task of reversing the damage Stalin had inflicted on the country.

In her book *Malevolent Nurture*, Deborah Willis notes that "during the 1930s and 1940s in Stalin's Soviet Union, leadership fractured at all levels, not only within Stalin's 'inner circle' but also within local and regional party machines ... As power oscillated between different factions, purges were carried out in the name of Stalin, 'Father of the Country, The Great and Wise Teacher, the Friend of Mankind,' against the antifathers and betraying sons who had perverted the Socialist program, the 'enemies with party cards.' "

If that sounds familiar, it may be because Saddam liked to be called "The Anointed One,

Glorious Leader, Direct Descendant of the Prophet, President of Iraq, Chairman of its Revolutionary Command Council, Field Marshal of its Armies, Doctor of its Laws and Great Uncle to all its peoples." Like Stalin, Saddam painted himself as a benevolent ruler and hero to his people while engaging in unspeakably vile atrocities in secret. It is no wonder that the Butcher of Baghdad's favorite movie was *The Godfather*.

But as evil as Saddam was, other members of his family may have been even worse — especially his two sons, Uday and Qusay. It was reported that as infants the two boys were allegedly given disarmed hand grenades to play with and that their father often brought them to the torture chamber with him to watch as prisoners were electrocuted, impaled on iron stakes or had their fingers chopped off.

In his biography *Saddam Hussein — The Politics of Revenge*, Palestinian author Said Aburish describes how the mother of a classmate of the brothers recalled that "Uday was loud and vulgar while Qusay was quiet and calculating." The book goes on to say, "in reality the boys were no different from the relations of other Middle East dictators. Their lack of proper upbringing is another testimony that even in Baathist Iraq, ideology was only skin-deep and family connections have always taken precedence."

Uday, the oldest, developed a reputation as a playboy who alienated many in Saddam's inner circle. He was also extraordinarily greedy for power and thought nothing of raping a woman if she resisted his advances. In one incident, related by an Iraqi defector, Uday accosted a newly-married couple in a park and had his guards drag the woman to a hotel room, where he raped her as the guards looked on from another room. Every bit as bloodthirsty as his father, Uday was a cold-blooded killer who took great delight in mutilating and murdering those he disfavored.

Uday Saddam Hussein al-Tikriti was born in 1964 to his mother Sajida, one of Saddam's wives who also happened to be his first cousin. In 1984 he was given the responsibility of overseeing the Iraqi National Olympic Committee and went to work on Iraqi athletes who did not measure up to his impossibly high standards.

Uday maintained his own prison at Iraq's Olympic complex, complete with guard towers and machine guns. There have been reports of many instances where Uday subjected losing athletes to beatings with iron bars, imprisoned them for months, chained them to walls in painful positions for days on end, dragged them across pavement until they were soaked in their own blood and then immersed them in raw sewage so that their wounds would become infected.

In May 2001, Saad Keis Naoman, an Iraqi soccer player who defected to Europe, recounted the horror of being second-best on Uday's team. He said that he and his roommates were beaten until their backs were raw and bloody, then made to sleep on their stomachs in a tiny jail cell at al-Radwaniya prison. Another Iraqi soccer player, Sharar Haydar Mohamad al-Hadithi, also reported being tortured when his team's Olympic efforts fell short of Uday's expectations. And members of the Iraqi national football team reported that in 1997 they were tortured and beaten on Uday's orders because he was displeased with their level of play.

Like his father, Uday would not tolerate any sort of contradiction or refusal to play by his rules. In one account, he had arranged a party for Suzanne Mubarak, the wife of Egyptian president Hosni Mubarak. As the celebration went on in downtown Baghdad on the banks of the Tigris River, another party was under way on the nearby Island of Pigs. It was being held by Kamel Hanna Jajo, a member of Saddam's inner circle who often procured women for the dictator and acted as one of his official food tasters. When Jajo and his fellow revelers began firing AK-47 rounds into the air, Uday became annoyed and crossed the river to ask him to stop. When another round was fired later, Uday crossed the river once again and bludgeoned Jajo to death.

When he realized he would face Saddam's wrath, Uday tried to commit suicide by taking an overdose of sleeping pills, but succeeded only in sickening himself. In their book *Out of the Ashes*, Andrew and Patrick Cockburn write, "As his stomach was being pumped, Saddam arrived in the emergency room, pushed the doctors aside and hit Uday in the face, shouting, 'Your blood will flow like my friend's!'" Saddam later softened his stance, but in a vivid instance of the pot calling the kettle black, he chastised his son: "Your behavior, Uday, is bad and there can be no worse than yours ... We want to know what kind of person you are. Are you a politician, a trader, a people's leader or a playboy? You must know that you have done nothing for this homeland or this people. The opposite is true." Uday was punished by being banished to Switzerland for a year, but the Swiss expelled him from the country after only six months when he became involved in fraud and money laundering.

Fully aware of the power of the press, Saddam's evil son weaseled his way into many of Iraq's major communication channels over the years — he even established his own newspaper, radio station and TV station. In 2000 he was elected to the Iraqi National Assembly, although in typical fashion, he didn't show up to claim his seat until eight months later. By most accounts a raving drunk, Uday had a penchant for designing his own bizarre clothing, including at least one suit that he created to match one of his luxury cars, which was bright red with white stripes.

At one stage, Uday had become impressed with Ismail Hussain, an Iraqi singer who had lost a leg in the Gulf War, and he regularly invited him to sing at his palace. "At the parties," reported Hussain, who now lives in Toronto, "I would be performing and Uday would climb on the stage with a gun and start shooting at the ceiling. Everyone would drop down, terrified. I was used to being around bigger weapons than Uday's Kalashnikov, so I would just keep on singing. Sometimes at these parties there would be dozens of women and only five or six men. Uday insists that everyone get drunk with him. He would interrupt my performance, get on stage with a big glass of cognac for himself and one for me. He would insist that I drink all of it with him. When he gets really drunk, out come the guns. His friends are all terrified of him, because he can have them imprisoned or killed. I saw him once get angry with one of his friends. He kicked the man in the ass so hard that his boot flew off. The man ran over and retrieved the boot and then tried to put it back on Uday's foot, with Uday cursing him all the while."

Understandably, Uday's lavish lifestyle and

despicable tactics earned him plenty of enemies within Iraq. So it came as no surprise to many when he was ambushed and shot by two gunmen in 1996, just a block away from his brother Qusay's secret police enclave. In what could have been a scene from a mob movie, Uday was hit several times, sustaining bullet wounds in his leg, arm and stomach, before the would-be assassins made off into the night. Although he was lucky enough to survive the attack, his injuries resulted in constant pain as well as a permanent and pronounced limp.

That may be one reason why most Mideast experts considered Qusay the sociopath to watch. Saddam's younger son, though quieter and more calculating, was by most accounts even more dangerous than Uday, whom experts pointed out had become an embarrassment to Saddam. Qusay was in charge of Iraq's security and intelligence agencies, and the head of both the Republican Guard and the elite Special Republican Guard. As Saddam's right-hand man and executioner, Qusay made sure anyone who showed signs of disloyalty to his father was dealt with swiftly and brutally.

Qusay Saddam Hussein al-Tikriti was born in 1966. Unlike Uday, he always made it a point to keep an extremely low profile, no doubt in order to mask his malicious activities. Though much less is known about him than his flamboyant brother as a result, the human rights organization Indict unearthed enough wrongdoings to brand him as a carbon copy of his vicious father.

- After an uprising against Saddam following the Gulf War of 1991, Qusay led his Republican Guard in the torture and mass execution of the rebels.
- He initiated attacks on Shiite and Marsh Arab Iraqi civilians in the south.
- He was instrumental in the continuing deportation, disappearance and murder of ethnic and religious minorities.
- In the past few years he ordered periodic "prison cleansing," in which several thousand inmates of Iraqi jails were put to death.
- He reportedly condoned the use of torture and rape as interrogation methods within his internal security agencies.

Indict reports these especially gruesome eyewitness accounts:

"On several occasions I saw Qusay Saddam Hussein walk along the row of cells, open the slot in the door and spray what I believe to be something like mustard gas into the cell ... The bodies of the dead were bloated by the gas. They foamed at the mouth and were bleeding from the eyes ... The prisoners were screaming. I remember one of them was only about 12 years old. I remember

Qusay shouting something like 'Put this bastard in — he's a member of the [X] family.' The little boy was screaming. He was already bleeding from previous beatings. Qusay killed him along with all the others ... The little boy screamed out, 'I am sorry, I don't want to die, I want my father.' Qusay said, 'Your father is in the cell next door,' which was true. Qusay then proceeded to spray him with gas and he died after about 10 minutes of agony. We could hear them screaming ... I estimate that Qusay Saddam Hussein personally murdered between 1,200-1,300 people during this period."

"Qusay Saddam Hussein went into the torture room ... screaming ... 'I'll put an end to you with my own hands.' [The prisoner] was brought back into the cell with his right foot covered in filthy bandages. It had been cut off during his torture ... the amputation had been carried out with a power saw during his torture under the direct supervision of Qusay Saddam Hussein ... it had not been done cleanly and it had taken some time to cut the foot off."

"There was a machine designed for shredding plastic. Men were dropped into it and we were again made to watch. Sometimes they went in head first and died quickly. Sometimes they were put in feet first and died screaming. It was horrible. I saw 30 people die like this. Their remains would be placed in plastic bags and we were told they would be used as fish food ... On one occasion, I saw Qusay Saddam Hussein personally supervising these murders."

To show how proud he was of the monster he brought into the world, Saddam recently directed Iraq's National Security Council to appoint Qusay as his successor. The Kuwaiti daily newspaper *al-Watan* published the Council's contingency plan:

"Considering the present situation in Iraq, and the serious threats from the U.S., Britain and other parties in particular, which want to eliminate the Iraqi leadership represented in the person of President Saddam Hussein, the Baath Party and its leaders, and [considering] the emergence of western covetous intentions toward Iraq and its resources; Iraq — leadership and people — must defend itself by taking measures to undermine this possible aggression by cooperating with the honorable and goodhearted sons of the Arab nation and friends around the world.

"Therefore, the 'National Security Council' decided to implement a plan called 'Decisive Reaction' based on the principles of the glorious July Revolution and the spirit of the Arab Socialist Baath Party, to fight back globalization and to confront the danger looming over our people from the West, the plan calls for:

"In case any harm or ill-fate befalls President Saddam Hussein personally, the leadership will revert automatically to comrade Qusay Saddam Hussein, who is in charge of the Republican Guard and the Republican Guard/Special Units. He will be vested with the same absolute authorities that President Saddam Hussein has in leading the country, the cabinet, and the army. Comrade Izzat Ibrahiim al-Dori will assume the responsibility for the party apparatus, while comrade Taha Yassin Ramadham and comrade Tariq Aziz will be responsible for assisting Qusay Saddam Hussein in governing the country. This arrangement will continue until the situation stabilizes. An [official] State Decree will follow."

Qusay's position as Saddam's successor was apparently a sore point with Uday, who'd had to watch his brother become the second most powerful man in Iraq while he hobbled around on crutches for three years following his assassination attempt. Despite Qusay's growing power, however, he was also targeted for assassination in 2002, when a Shiite opposition group known as The Supreme Revolutionary Council attacked him in Baghdad. Qusay had just left the presidential palace and was about to get into a car bound for Iraqi General Intelligence headquarters when his handlers suddenly directed him to a different vehicle. Moments later the original car exploded, killing Qusay's driver and three of his bodyguards. His would-be assassins were never captured but, unlike Uday, Qusay escaped unharmed.

Saddam's sons were by no means the only rats in the Iraqi government cellar. After Uday and Qusay, the most notorious Iraqi official was Ali Hasan al-Majid, also known as "Chemical Ali" and "The Butcher of Kurdistan" for his role in gassing Iraq's Kurdish population in 1988. As a member of the Revolutionary Command Council and a trusted presidential adviser, al-Majid was largely responsible for many of the war crimes that Saddam's corrupt regime committed during its hellish rule.

An army motorcycle messenger until the Baath revolution in 1968, al-Majid quickly rose through the ranks primarily because he was Saddam's first cousin. In 1988 Saddam put him in charge of the armed forces for the al-Anfal Campaign in which Kurdish Rebels were slaughtered by the thousands. When he met with Kurdish leaders who accused him of murdering 182,000 civilians, al-Majid hotly denied the charge, protesting that "it couldn't have been more than 100,000." He was also caught on audiotape weighing in on the value of Kurdish lives, saying, "Am I supposed to keep them in good shape? No, I shall bury them with bulldozers."

When Saddam invaded Kuwait in 1991, he made al-Majid governor of the occupied country, a position he held for five months. But in that short time he wrought untold destruction and bloodshed on Kuwait, torturing and murdering thousands, many of whom are still unaccounted for.

Kenneth Roth, head of the New York-based Human Rights Watch organization, spoke of al-Majid on the group's Web site, stating that "he has been involved in some of Iraq's worst war crimes" and, in what might be the understatement of the year, added that "bringing him to justice is an essential priority."

Saddam employed many others who deserve a military tribunal, including Muhammad Hamza al-Zubaydi, former Iraqi Prime Minister and current Deputy Prime Minister. Dubbed the "Shia Thug" for aiding al-Majid in violently putting down the Shiite uprising after the first Gulf War, al-Zubaydi was caught on video kicking and beating Shiite prisoners of war. Other Iraqi officers long overdue for justice included Watban Ibrahim al-Hasan al-Tikriti, Saddam's half-brother and advisor, who was accused of mass executions and torture during the Kurdish uprising, and Sab'awi Ibrahim al-Hasan al-Tikriti, another half-brother and former director of intelligence responsible for multiple human-rights violations including murder, torture, rape and deportation.

One of the most bizarre incidents involving Saddam's inner circle took place in 1995 after two of his sons-in-law became turncoats. Lieutenant

General Hussein Kamel al-Majid was not only married to one of Saddam's daughters, but was also the Minister of Military Industries, which meant he was responsible for all of Iraq's extensive chemical, biological and nuclear programs. Hussein defected to Jordan with his brother, Lieutenant Colonel Saddam Kamel al-Majid, and exposed the Great Uncle's reign of terror to the world. Hussein had hoped that the West would use this intelligence to take Saddam down and intended to persuade them to install him as Saddam's successor. However, the two sons-in-law were no angels themselves. Hussein had bragged of making one of his aides drink gasoline and then shooting him in the stomach, while his brother-in-law took great delight in recounting the time he literally beat a Republican Guard soldier's brains out. When Hussein realized that his succession was not an option and that the West was interested only in the intelligence he could provide, he became depressed and homesick. Baghdad soon contacted the traitors with offers of clemency and the two returned to Iraq. What happened next was not surprising.

Upon their return, Saddam summoned them to one of his palaces and demanded they sign divorce papers. According to Abbas al-Janabi, Uday's former personal secretary who was present at the time and later defected to Europe, the brothers refused to sign. Saddam gave them two days to reconsider, but that night Uday and other members of Saddam's family surrounded the house where the two were staying and began shooting.

"It was a massacre," al-Janabi reported. During a 13-hour gunfight, Hussein was wounded and staggered out of the house, where he was riddled with bullets by Uday's henchmen, who continued to fire even after Hussein had fallen dead on the ground.

To anyone with a shred of humanity, the appalling brutality of Saddam's regime is revolting. Unfortunately, in the world of murderous despots his loathsome methods of maintaining power are not unusual. To understand how Saddam became a man without a conscience, unable to trust even those closest to him and more than willing to destroy his own countrymen, you have to start at the very beginning, in a small village in central Iraq.

CHAPTER 2

A TRADITION OF TERROR

odern-day Iraq lies in the area once known as Mesopotamia, considered to be the cradle of civilization. The name Mesopotamia is a Greek word which means "land between the rivers." Referring to the great Tigris and Euphrates rivers that flow through what is called the Fertile Crescent, this region is known as the birthplace of agriculture. The area's mild climate, rich soil and abundant water supply made it a perfect place for early settlers to flourish. More than 6,000 years ago, great civilizations rose from that lush river valley and brought the world inventions such as the plow, the wheel and writing. Biblical scholars even pinpoint Mesopotamia as the site of the Garden of Eden.

But the area's riches also made it a tempting target and over its thousands of years of recorded history, Iraq has been repeatedly overrun by conquering armies, which brought a tradition of violence to the realm. With its long history of conflict, intrigue and strife, the country's residents have found themselves living on a battleground time after time, until the concept of peace has become a distant dream.

The earliest known inhabitants of Mesopotamia, the Sumerians, lived and worked in the first city-states on the planet. They invented cuneiform, a method of translating speech into writing by pressing characters into soft clay tablets with a sharp stick. The tablets were then baked to preserve the text. The Sumerians also invented mathematics and geometry; they established 360 degrees as the circumference of a circle and are credited with creating the 60-minute hour.

Sargon the Great established Mesopotamia's military tradition when he gathered an army and began overthrowing the Sumerian city-states around 2300 B.C. One of the world's first empire-builders, he was soon expanding his dynasty into nearby areas such as Syria and what is now Iran, and for a time all was well. But in the tradition of the territory, the latter part of his reign was marked by unrest and rebellion.

The end of Sargon's rule paved the way for Hammurabi, who was one of the first rulers to establish a code of laws. The Code of Hammurabi is widely regarded as the model for the modern legal system and included the concept of "an eye for an eye." Hammurabi ruled from Babylon, about 50 miles south of present-day Baghdad, and although his reign was marked by literary activity and other advances, he was also known as "Hammurabi, the strong warrior, the destroyer of his foes, the hurricane of battle."

Hammurabi was succeeded by Nebuchadnezzar, builder of the famed Hanging Gardens of Babylon. King Nebuchadnezzar II was responsible for many improvements and building projects such as Babylon's Ishtar gate, but, like his predecessors, he was also an imperialistic dynasty-builder.

In 587 B.C. Nebuchadnezzar attacked Jerusalem to put down a rebellion there, destroyed the temple of King Solomon and led most of Jerusalem's citizens back to Babylon in chains. Eventually Nebuchadnezzar's empire stretched from the Mediterranean Sea to the Persian Gulf.

In the mid-6th century B.C., Cyrus the Great conquered Babylon and in 331 B.C. Alexander the Great took over, entering the walled city without a fight. For the next thousand years or so, control of Mesopotamia seesawed between the Persians, Greeks and Romans. In 634 A.D. the first Islamic incursion took place in the area when 18,000 troops under the command of general Khalid ibn al-Walid, known as the "Sword of Islam," marched into Mesopotamia. The Muslim warriors demanded that their captives either convert or pay a tribute in order to stay alive.

In the year 762 A.D., the city of Baghdad was established and eventually became known as one of the world's great centers of learning and culture. But Baghdad's Golden Age wouldn't last. In 1258 A.D. a horde of Mongols led by one of Genghis Khan's grandsons tore through Baghdad, reducing the city to rubble and killing nearly a million people. He dumped thousands of books into the Tigris River and destroyed its advanced canal system, ruining the local agricultural economy. The Mongols, Turks and Persians fought for control of Mesopotamia for the next few centuries until the Ottoman Empire finally conquered the disputed land in 1640.

The Ottoman Turks retained control until 1914, when the British invaded Mesopotamia to protect their oil interests. In five months, England lost 23,000 troops and another 10,000 were forced to surrender. After such a huge setback, it took three more years of fighting before Britain was in firm control of Baghdad. After capturing the city, Lieutenant General Sir Stanley Maude, commander of the British forces, tried to reassure the conquered that his motives were pure in a proclamation to the people of Baghdad: "Our armies do not come into your cities and lands as conquerors or enemies but as liberators. It is (Britain's) wish that you should prosper even as in the past, when your lands were fertile, when your ancestors gave the world literature, science and art and when Baghdad City was one of the wonders of the world."

But they were empty words. Although Britain had promised the Arab residents their independence, after seizing power it instead occupied the area after being awarded stewardship at the Paris Peace Conference. That sparked a 1920 rebellion, which the British put down with aerial bombardment — the first use of bombs on Baghdad and a foreshadowing of things to come.

The British set to work defining the boundaries of what would become Iraq, planting the seeds of its future turmoil, according to most Mideast experts. In the map of Iraq drawn up by British officials (including Winston Churchill), the country would be composed of three former Ottoman districts: the northern area occupied by the Kurds; the central portion, which was composed mostly of Sunni Arabs and included Baghdad, and the southern part, which was predominantly Shiite. Composed of groups which were often at war with each other, the British created a country that was unstable by nature.

Britain then established a puppet government, presiding over an election that propelled King

Faisal to the throne by a landslide. Of course, in what would later become a Saddam tradition, his was the only name on the ballot. In 1932 Iraq was finally declared independent, joined the League of Nations and began exporting oil two years later.

Faisal was able to keep the country afloat for a few years — after all, he was a war hero, having fought against the Turks with the legendary T. E. Lawrence, also known as Lawrence of Arabia. But after Faisal died in 1933, it wasn't long before Iraq experienced its first modern coup in 1936. The year after that, a son was born to Subha Tulfah and Hussein al-Majid in the small town of al-Ouja, near Tikrit in central Iraq. They named the baby Saddam, meaning "the one who confronts."

In his book *Saddam: King of Terror*, British journalist Con Coughlin describes life for the young Saddam in al-Ouja as being a lot like life in the Old West: harsh and lawless. The future dictator's father disappeared shortly after he was born and he was raised by a cruel stepfather known as "Hassan the Liar" who beat him mercilessly and refused to send him to school. Instead, Saddam was made to tend sheep and perform menial tasks in the family's stick-and-mud house. At night his parents sent him out to steal what he could from nearby farms. His mother was an evil-tempered woman whose only known occupation was the village fortuneteller and some accounts say she also dabbled in prostitution. As a boy Saddam was tormented by the village bullies who called him a bastard and son of a whore, so he took to carrying an iron bar everywhere he went for protection. One story relates the time Saddam heated the bar until it glowed red-hot and then used it to split open an animal's stomach.

Some accounts say that Saddam was caught stealing and sent to a detention center and others claim he was sexually abused by his stepfather. Villagers remembered hearing Hassan often shouting, "I don't want him, the son of a dog!" What is known is that Saddam's uncle Khairallah Tulfah rescued him from his barbaric stepfather when he was 10 years old and took him to live in Baghdad. Tulfah was an army officer, an Arab nationalist and a big fan of Adolf Hitler, and he instilled a similar admiration for Nazism in the young Saddam. In fact, the uncle was jailed by the British for six years after taking part in a pro-Nazi revolt in Baghdad. Tulfah hated Jews, Communists and Persians, who were mostly Shiites, and even published a pamphlet entitled *Three Whom God Should Not Have Created: Persians, Jews and Flies*. His prejudices were eagerly absorbed by the young Saddam.

When his uncle was finally released, the illiterate Saddam was finally able to begin his education while living with Tulfah in Tikrit. Unfortunately for the future dictator, his poor background and complete lack of social skills became the butt of jokes among his classmates, and while in school he often got into fights. It didn't help that the 14-year-old Saddam was put into a class with 5-year-olds. It's said that after rising to power, Saddam came back to Tikrit to destroy his former tormentors.

After suffering a beating by of one of his teachers, Saddam paid the instructor a late-night visit. When the teacher's brother opened the door, Saddam shot him and then galloped away on his horse. The teacher called the police, but was unable to prove Saddam was the culprit and soon moved away from Tikrit.

One of his contemporaries recalled that the school's headmaster decided to expel the trouble-making Saddam at that point so, like a Mafia Don, Saddam paid him a visit as well. The source said that "when he heard about this decision, Saddam came to his headmaster's room and threatened him with death. He said, 'I will kill you if you do not withdraw your threat to expel me.'" The expulsion plan was dropped, a lesson to Saddam that threatening violence was a great way to ensure that he intimidated his enemies and got his way.

Childhood friend Ibrahim Zobedi recalls that

"when (Saddam) tried to kill his teacher in 1952, his uncle began respecting him. He realized that killing was the right way to go about getting respect from his family. This later encouraged him to try and assassinate the president of Iraq. The whole family and the atmosphere in the village was not normal. Normally, if you steal, people treat you badly. But in al-Ouja if you steal they respect you and if you kill they respect you more."

Zobedi remembers going fishing with Saddam — using dynamite. "The fishermen would always tell us to make sure our stomach and legs were out of the water," Zobedi recalled. "Of course, Saddam would do the opposite and stand in the river up to his chest."

Zobedi also recalled the day he decided to leave Iraq. It was the last time he saw Saddam, after he became vice president in 1973. "He was sitting there," said Zobedi, "and when I looked at him he looked away. I thought, 'He doesn't want me. He wants to be a big player and he wants no friends from his childhood who remember when he was nothing — that he had no talent and was nothing special.' And after I left, I found out that many of his childhood friends were killed in car accidents or at night. I was right — he wanted to get rid of those old friends."

In 1955 Saddam enrolled in a Baghdad high school, and in his late teens he joined the Baath

Party, which had been formed in 1947 to create a united Arab state and get rid of the colonial influence that had controlled Iraq for so long. The British puppet government was fading in the face of intense Iraqi opposition and the Baathists planned to use any means necessary to seize power, making the party a great fit for the soulless Saddam.

The Baath Party put Saddam to work as an assassin and in 1958 he made his first hit on a leading Communist named Saadoun al-Tikriti. That same year a senior Iraqi general named Abdul Karim Qassem seized power in a bloody coup that took the lives of the entire royal family. Baathist officials immediately decided that Qassem must be assassinated — and who better to do their dirty work than the now-veteran killer Saddam Hussein?

By all accounts, the assassination attempt went terribly wrong. The stories vary, but the accepted version says that Saddam had planned to use a car to block the street and intercept Qassem's motorcade, catching the leader in an ambush. But when the time came to pull in front of the motorcade, the driver couldn't find the keys and Saddam and his henchmen desperately fired on Qassem's limousine from the sidewalk as it sped past. Qassem's driver was killed in the blaze of gunfire and the president was wounded, but

Saddam's men also caught each other in the crossfire. Saddam was hit in his left leg by a stray bullet and he may have accidentally shot and killed fellow assassin Abdel Wahab Goreiri.

The official Iraqi account says that Saddam carved the bullet out of his leg with a pair of scissors after being carried to safety and then escaped on horseback. It also describes his swim across the Tigris River to his boyhood town of al-Ouja and his escape to Syria dressed as a woman wearing a burqa. Whether or not the account is true, the story was later made into a six-hour movie called *The Long Days*, which became required viewing for all Iraqis after Saddam seized power.

What is certain is that the assassination attempt was a spectacular failure that made Saddam and his cronies look like buffoons. Surprisingly, the bungled operation didn't get Saddam into hot water with the Baath Party, but it did force him to spend nearly four years in exile, first in Damascus and then in Cairo, where he studied law. While in Egypt he also became engaged to his first cousin Sajida.

Saddam sneaked back into Iraq in 1963 and was soon arrested and thrown in jail for his botched assassination attempt. While he was in prison, big changes were taking place in Iraq. His cousin Ahmed Hassan al-Bakr, who was also

from Tikrit, became the leader of the Iraqi Baath
Party and when Saddam reportedly escaped from
jail in 1966, he was made deputy-chairman of the
Revolutionary Command Council and became
al-Bakr's right-hand man. The two set to work
planning the overthrow of the current regime.

On July 17, 1968, Baathist tanks burst through
the gates of the presidential palace. According to
Saddam's autobiography, he was in the vanguard,
leading the attack from the front as he blasted
away at the opposing forces from the lead tank.
The Baath Party was soon in control of Baghdad,
and al-Bakr became president of Iraq. For his
contributions to the party, Saddam was named
vice president and head of security and it wasn't
long before he had established himself as the
power behind al-Bakr's throne. One of his first
acts in his new capacity was to announce the
exposure and destruction of a Zionist spy ring.
Saddam arranged a public hanging for the 14 ring
members that included 11 Jews. The bodies were
left hanging for days in Baghdad's Liberation
Square, which came to be known as the Square of
the Hanged.

As a high-ranking Baath Party member, Saddam
steeped himself in the teachings of its founder,
Michel Aflaq. A Syrian intellectual and political
activist, Aflaq had formed an organization known
as the Movement of Arab Renaissance in

Damascus in 1940, which became the Baath Party in 1947. Aflaq chose the name Baath because it meant "renaissance" in Arabic, but the party would become much better known for its appalling brutality. Although Aflaq was a Greek Orthodox Christian, he believed that Islam gives Arabs "the most brilliant picture of their language and literature, and the grandest part of their national history." Although not an Arab himself, Aflaq considered Arabs to be a master race that must constantly struggle to protect itself from the influence of outsiders.

Aflaq's teachings became the foundation of Saddam's evil empire. Just as Hitler's belief in a master race had done in the 1940s, Aflaq's assertion that Arabs were superior and above man's laws helped Saddam establish a culture of violence within the Baath Party. One particularly twisted piece of Baathist propaganda stated that "every party, including the ABSP (Arab Socialist Baath Party), constitutes a minority in proportion to its population ... But when it represents, by its will and daily conduct, the people's will, when its acts correspond to the people's objectives, in present and future calculations, then it constitutes a majority."

With that sort of backward logic, it's no wonder Saddam was able to justify any act of violence, no matter how obscene. Aflaq taught that Arabs could only ascend to a dominant state through perpetual revolution and conflict, and Saddam repeatedly parroted those teachings in his writings and speeches. On the topic of struggle he said, "That is why a revolution has no beginning and no end; it is not like a war and its soldiers must not profit from its spoils. It is something continuous, it is a message to life and the human being is only the bearer of the message.

"The revolution chooses its enemies and we say chooses its enemies because some enemies are chosen by it from among the people who run up against its program and who intend to harm it. The revolution has its eyes wide open. Throughout all its stages the revolution will remain capable of performing its role courageously and precisely without hesitation or panic, once it takes action to crush the pockets of the counter-revolution."

Aflaq and Saddam also believed that the truth had to take a back seat to the party's immediate needs, since the party and the revolution were all-important, not the actual facts. In a speech to a group of history teachers, Saddam said, "The Baathist must never deal with history and all other intellectual and social questions in this way ... The writing of history must take on the same specificity as our Baathist way; in other words, the writing of Arab history should be from our point of view with an emphasis on analysis and not on realistic story telling."

Saddam later asserted that even the Baath Party's own founding principles could be ignored if the situation demanded it. He explained that Baath Party members should be guided only by the needs of the future, which could change at any time: "Our decisive criterion when there are various alternatives and visions in front of us, is not the modest picture, but the highest and purest state. This is what distinguishes the Baath regime from all other regimes."

With his doctrine of might-makes-right, Saddam increasingly appointed his relatives and friends from Tikrit to leadership positions as he consolidated his power behind the scenes. In 1972, President al-Bakr signed a friendship pact with the Soviet Union, which began supplying Iraq with arms, many of which are still used by the military to this day. He also nationalized Iraq's oil industry, and seized oil fields from Dutch, British and U.S. companies. The Soviet Union immediately took up the slack by offering their help to Iraq's oil industry.

As vice president, one of Saddam's responsibilities was to keep the Kurds in northern Iraq under control. In 1974 fighting broke out between Kurdish rebels and Iraqi forces, just as it had for decades. Because the Kurds were supported by both the

United States and Iran at the time, the battle ended in a draw. But in 1975 Saddam persuaded Iran to withdraw its support and when the U.S. also withdrew, the Kurdish revolt collapsed. Saddam's troops slaughtered many Kurds in the aftermath, while others fled into neighboring countries.

The Kurds felt the sting of Saddam's de facto rule again the next year, when he began a countrywide "Arabization" program in Iraq, which was actually an attempt at ethnic cleansing. Many were forcibly deported and 4,000 villages were destroyed, including their crops, trees, animals and water supplies. Half a million Kurds were sent to labor camps in the purge.

Within the Baath Party, the paranoid vice president was busy getting rid of potential rivals by declaring one conspiracy after another. Historian Charles Tripp recounted some of them: "There was the so-called 'Communist conspiracy' of 1978 whereby many of the leftists in the party were purged, killed, arrested, disappeared. And in 1979, there was the so-called 'Syrian conspiracy,' where many of the Arab nationalists in the party were equally disposed of through denunciations, arrests and executions."

By 1979, Iraqi President Ahmed Hassan al-Bakr's health was failing and Saddam persuaded him — in most accounts by force — to step down, leaving Saddam as Iraq's sole ruler. In *Saddam:*

King of Terror, Con Coughlin described how the outgoing president was made to appear on television and declare that he was willingly abdicating his throne, which most Iraq-watchers very much doubt.

Five days after Saddam's takeover, he called all senior Baath Party members in Iraq to a special conference, but none of them could have guessed just what kind of meeting it would be. After the thousand or so delegates assembled at the al-Khuld convention center in Baghdad, the newly appointed vice president began to read a statement. There had been a "painful and atrocious plot" against Saddam's government, he said, and what was more, the backstabbers were present in that very room.

As a wave of shock and fear swept through the audience, Saddam slowly rose from his seat and took the podium. After telling the assembled crowd he had evidence of a vast conspiracy against him, he brought out Muhie Abdul Hussein Mashhadi, who had been secretary-general of the Revolutionary Command Council until he took the courageous but ill-advised step of opposing Saddam's presidency. Mashhadi had been tortured for his breach of faith and now he stood and recited a list of names, dates and places where the supposed plot was hatched.

When he was through, Saddam once again took

the dais and denounced the fabricated conspiracy, then said: "The people whose names I am going to read out should repeat the party slogan and leave the hall." As the list was read, the accused were led from the room by armed guards while the remaining delegates sweated. When the list was done, 66 high-ranking Baath Party officials had been branded as traitors.

As the remainder of the crowd realized they were safe, they leapt to their feet and began singing Saddam's praises while he puffed away on his cigar. Some even wept openly at being spared by the Great Uncle. At the end of the meeting Saddam joined the audience and offered the delegates positions on the firing squads that would soon be executing the 66 so-called traitors. In what would become another Saddam tradition, the entire event was videotaped so that Saddam could broadcast it as a warning to his enemies.

The video also features footage of the executions. Coughlin described the video footage of the executions as "an orgy of killing" in which "the camera shows the condemned men kneeling with blindfolds over their eyes, their wrists tied behind their backs. The camera then closes in showing a hand holding a gun, which fires a shot into the temple. The victims jerk and then crumple over, blood oozing from their heads in the dust. In some cases the shootings prove inaccurate, leaving

the victims still alive. Because some of the execu-
tioners were not professional gunmen, they had
either missed the intended target or had lost their
nerve at the last minute. In these instances the
camera shows a professional executioner apply-
ing the coup de grace with a pistol shot to the
head."

Saddam had been president for less than a year
when he made his first major blunder. Six months
before he came to power, the Shah of Iran had
been overthrown and Iran was now led by the
Ayatollah Khomeni. Saddam felt the new extrem-
ist government in Iran was a threat to his country,
especially when the Ayatollah and his cronies
began to make statements indicating that they felt
"all countries around the Gulf were historically
part of Iranian territory" and "We must ... export
our revolution to other parts of the world and
renounce the concept of keeping the Revolution
within our own boundaries."

To test Iran's resolve and size up the country's air
defenses, Saddam began violating Iranian air
space in 1979. Iran responded by launching
assaults on a few Iraqi cities in a bid to terrorize
their inhabitants. On April 1, 1980, a bomb
exploded in a group of students at Baghdad's
University of Mustansiriya, killing several people.
Soon after, attempts were made to kill Tariq Aziz,
Iraq's Deputy Prime Minister, and Latif Nasif

Jasim, the Iraqi Minister of Culture and Information. Four days after the university bombing, another bomb blew up in a funeral procession for those killed in the previous blast, launching a countrywide search for Iranian sympathizers and activists.

Saddam saw the Iranian attacks as not only a direct threat to his presidency but also an embarrassment. Although publicly saying he had no designs on Iranian territory, Saddam terminated the Algiers Treaty of 1975 that had established the boundaries between the two countries. On Sept. 21, 1980, Iraqi troops crossed the border into Iran and began shelling Iranian cities, while the Iraqi air force dropped bombs on Teheran and other urban centers. In retaliation, Iranian aircraft bombed Iraqi oil fields near Basra, bringing the entire Iraqi oil industry to a grinding halt.

The United Nations Security Council immediately tried to get the two countries to agree to a cease-fire, but when Iran's prime minister appeared before the council on October 17, he claimed that Iraq had shelled hospitals and schools, killed schoolchildren and babies and was plundering and devastating Iran. He was quoted as saying that "the spectacle of dead and wounded, which I have seen with my own eyes, would move the most heartless of men."

But Iraq maintained that it was simply protecting itself from Iranian attacks and defending its national territory. In addition, Saddam claimed that he was fighting for all Arab countries against Persian domination. But in reality, Saddam was power-mad. Still bursting with overconfidence from his takeover of Iraq and filled with Arab nationalism, he thought there was no one who could stop him. With the absolute authority he held in Iraq, there was certainly no one in that terrorized country who would try. And given his gigantic ego, after taking the first steps toward war, there was no way he would back down.

Iran had long supported various Shiite opposition groups within Iraq and, with the increased terrorist attacks against his officers, those groups felt the effects of Saddam's full fury. Shortly after the attempt on Tariq Aziz's life, Iraq's most prominent Shiite religious leader Ayatollah Muhammad Baqir al-Sadr was executed, along with his sister. Hundreds of Shiite political prisoners were shot to death before firing squads and even some Iraqi army officers were killed, accused of siding with the Iranians.

While Saddam had proven himself to be an expert at terrorism, the war with Iran showed him to be less than competent at commanding a battlefield. Unbelievably, within a week of the invasion of Iran and with military victory almost a foregone conclusion, Saddam commanded his troops to halt in their progress while he attempted to negotiate a settlement. It was yet another major blunder for the dictator. While Iran had no intention of bargaining with Saddam, the break gave the Teheran government time to build up its defenses and regroup while the Iraqi army waited in the desert, its morale plummeting.

As the days turned into weeks and months, Saddam's soldiers were subjected to the harsh desert climate and repeated guerrilla attacks on their positions and dissension began to stir in the ranks. Many soldiers defected, abandoning their weapons and willingly becoming prisoners of war to escape the brutal conditions. This filled the Iranian revolutionaries in Teheran with glee and they took little time in capitalizing on Saddam's lack of military skills.

In early 1981 Iran mounted a major counter-offensive, rooting out many of the Iraqi troops from their entrenched positions and sending them fleeing back toward Iraq. Later that year Iran began the tactic of simultaneously sending thousands of people swarming toward Iraqi positions, often overwhelming them even though Iranian losses were great. As the year continued and Iran made even more successful raids on Iraqi troops, Saddam sent Yasin Ramadan, his First Deputy Prime Minister, to tell Iran it might be willing to withdraw in stages. Iran responded by launching a series of all-out attacks called Operation Undeniable Victory that nearly drove Iraq completely out of Iran.

Saddam's problems continued to mount in 1981. He had commissioned French and Italian companies to build a nuclear reactor named Osirak two years earlier, supposedly to generate power but actually to supply fuel for Iraq's nuclear weapons program. Israel watched the construction with mounting apprehension, knowing that if Saddam gained atomic weapons, its future was dark indeed. On June 7, eight F-16s took off from Israel, each carrying a pair of 2,000-pound bombs. Escorted by two F-15s, the formation flew extremely low to avoid radar, its planes spaced in a pattern that would resemble a passenger airliner if it were somehow picked up on Iraqi screens. An hour and a half later, the squadron dropped its bombs on the reactor and in less than 80 seconds nothing was left but a smoking pile of rubble — another setback in Saddam's domination plans.

In May 1982, Iranian forces recaptured the city of Khorramshahr, which Iraqi soldiers had seized at the beginning of the war. Iran captured 12,000 prisoners of war and military equipment that had been left behind when Iraqi troops ran for their lives. Saddam had no choice but to pull back to the safety of his own border, further bolstering

Iranian morale. As the tide of war continued to turn against him, he became even more paranoid and self-delusional. In one 1982 Baath cabinet meeting, Riyadh Ibrahim Hussein, Iraq's Minister of Health, suggested that Saddam allow ex-President al-Bakr to negotiate a cease-fire, intimating that the dictator's attempts had been less than successful. "Let us go to the other room and discuss the matter further," Saddam told him. The two men walked into an adjoining room where Saddam shot and killed Hussein, then calmly returned to the meeting.

On the home front, Saddam's problems were still mounting. When the war began two years earlier, most of the soldiers in northern Iraq had been moved to the front lines, which left a power vacuum in the area. Now the Kurdish rebellion came surging back, aided and supplied by Iran. In 1983 the rebels helped Iranian forces capture an Iraqi border town. In retaliation, Iraqi troops swept into areas where relocated Kurds were living and abducted up to 12,000 Kurdish males from the age of 12 on up. They were never seen again.

As the war ground on, the economies of both Iraq and Iran began to suffer. Because they had pounded each other's oil fields to pieces, economic development in both countries had slowed and finally come to a standstill. In 1985 both nations began to import Scud-B rockets from Russia and immediately started lobbing them at each other's cities and industrial complexes. But the war really took a turn for the worse with the introduction of Iraq's weapons of mass destruction.

Saddam's weapons of choice were mustard gas and the nerve agent Tabun, originally developed by the Nazis. First used in World War I by the Germans, mustard gas is actually a liquid which is categorized as a blister agent that burns skin and causes blisters and severe respiratory distress. Victims begin to notice its effects in one to six hours after being exposed even to small amounts and can die from larger doses. The first symptoms include vomiting, blistered skin and eye irritation, followed by external and internal bleeding. As the gas permeates the lungs it attacks the bronchial tubes, stripping away the mucous membrane and making it impossible for the lungs to function.

Tabun is an odorless amber liquid that attacks the body's central nervous system. The first sign of exposure is a runny nose and tightness in the chest, along with a constriction of the pupils. Sufferers then begin having trouble breathing and may begin to drool and vomit. The later stages are marked by complete loss of bodily functions, causing uncontrolled vomiting, defecation and urination. Victims twitch and jerk, become comatose and suffocate due to convulsions.

The first use of gas against Iranian troops was in 1984, when Saddam's men found themselves unable to dislodge the forces from a swamp near Basra. Coughlin describes how Iraqi helicopters dumped chemical agents into enemy troop positions or sprayed them with the deadly mixture:

"The Iranians, who had no protective clothing, fell ill immediately. Within minutes they began vomiting a yellowish liquid and their skin turned red. By the time the medics reached the battlefield, some of the troops were already dead, their faces horribly blackened by the gas. Others had amber-colored blisters all over their bodies and were having trouble breathing."

By 1985 the Kurdish opposition in the north of Iraq had reached the boiling point and Saddam decided to take definitive action to suppress the rebels. He executed 8,000 Kurds who had been captured two years earlier, along with hundreds of other Kurdish opposition members, and revived his ethnic cleansing campaign. As Iranian forces advanced toward northern Iraq in 1987, Saddam realized many Kurds might well join them in the fight against his regime. To prevent that scenario, he sent his cousin Ali Hasan al-Majid, to address the problem.

In May the ruthless "Chemical Ali" directed an

attack on 20 Kurd-occupied communities with mustard gas, cyanide and Tabun. The following month he did the same to several Kurdish villages in Iran. But the incident that firmly established him as one of history's true monsters took place in March 1988, when it seemed the Iranians were about to launch a major push into Iraq. Al-Majid dispatched artillery and aircraft to bombard the Kurdish village of Halabja, but it was no ordinary attack.

When the first wave of shelling and bombing began, the village's inhabitants gathered their children and relatives and fled into bomb shelters, where they thought they were safe, at least for the moment. But the second wave of bombing included something else: hydrogen cyanide gas. In a radio interview, journalist Jeffrey Goldberg explained Ali's inhuman strategy:

"You have to understand something here that's so diabolically clever. The Iraqis knew that gas is heavier than air and would penetrate cellars and basements more effectively by launching a conventional artillery attack on the town for several hours. In other words, they knew that people would do what they always did during an artillery barrage and run to their basements. They were stuck in their basements and then [the Iraqis] launched the chemical weapons attack ... turning them, really, into gas chambers."

In fact, the gas Ali used was very similar to the chemicals used by the Nazis during the Holocaust. When the terrified residents realized what was happening, those who could still move grabbed their children and tried to flee downwind. Goldberg related the story of one survivor, Nouri Hama Ali, who led his family to Anab, a resettlement center for Kurds left homeless by Saddam's attacks:

"On the road to Anab, many of the women and children began to die. The chemical clouds were on the ground. They were heavy. We could see them." People were dying all around, he said. When a child could not go on, the parents, becoming hysterical with fear, abandoned him. "Many children were left on the ground, by the side of the road. Old people as well. They were running, then they would stop breathing and die."

When photographs of the piles of contorted corpses were broadcast around the world, viewers were horrified at the cruelty of Saddam's brutal regime. It was thought at the time that perhaps a few hundred people had died in the attack, but a later investigation showed that more than 5,000 villagers had met their deaths at Chemical Ali's hand. It was just one part of Saddam's extermination campaign he called al-Anfal (The spoils of war), a genocidal push to kill and displace the predominantly Kurdish citizens of northern Iraq.

The watchdog group Human Rights Watch estimates that between 50,000 and 100,000 human beings, many of them women and children, were murdered in 1988 alone.

In 1988 the war began to turn in Iraq's favor and, after a series of battlefield successes, Iran finally accepted the U.N.'s cease-fire terms in July. Both countries were in shambles, nearly bankrupt, pockmarked with bomb craters and barely fit for human habitation, but in Saddam's mind, he was the victor. He was, after all, still in power, having shown that he would use any means necessary to stay there. Just one question remained — who would be next on his hit list?

The watching group thought it was a freak col-
lision that killed between 60,000 and 100,000 human
beings, many of them women and children, were
gathered in one place.

. . . In fact, the was the so that in one city . . . one
city, where a very . . . . pestilential epidemic that
began spread in . . . . a certain center in just . . . .
both countries were in distances, may it benefit . . . . . contrasted with bombardments and being
in fit in misses, in reality, but in actuality . . . . .
. . . . before the crises . . the very approval and to prove
. . . . before crises and incapable and say secret was
. . . . . his city . . . . . and our first the invading . . . . . .
. . . . who would be settled, might just . . . .

CHAPTER 3

A STORM ON THE DESERT

Before the beginning of the war with Iran in 1980, Iraq's economy was prospering — it even boasted a $35 billion trade surplus. But according to Efraim Karsh and Lawrence Freedman in their book *The Gulf Conflict, 1990-1991: Diplomacy and War in the New World Order,* Iraq was nearly broke by the war's end. Saddam's massive miscalculation of Iran's strength had resulted in a foreign debt load of more than $80 billion, not including the cost of reconstructing the shattered nation, which some analysts estimated to be in the neighborhood of $230 billion.

Iraq's major creditor was Kuwait, on the shores of the Persian Gulf to the south. Kuwait had been Iraq's ally during the war, supplying loans to enable Saddam to buy weapons from Russia and generally helping to support his war effort. But by

1990 Iraq's oil fields were generating an income
of only $13 billion a year, barely enough to keep
Saddam's million or so troops and his military
infrastructure afloat, much less repay his debts.
True to his sociopathic nature, the dictator decided
that since he couldn't reduce his debt, he would
instead eliminate his creditors.

Saddam had always maintained that Kuwait
should have been a part of Iraq from the beginning, when the British were divvying up the
remains of the Ottoman Empire, and he planned
to use his argument as an excuse to invade the
country if Kuwait didn't agree to his demands. In
1989 Iraq approached Kuwait's prime minister
about retiring its debt, claiming that its "victory"
over Iran had been done for Arabs everywhere,
and that Iraq deserved a reward for its bravery.
But Kuwait insisted on payment, arguing that it
had lent the money in good faith and at the risk of
invoking the wrath of Iran.

In July 1990, American intelligence noted a
horde of Iraqi troops moving toward the Kuwaiti
border. Although Saddam was assuring the world
he would seek a negotiated settlement to his dis-
putes with the tiny country, at 2 a.m. on August 2
he sent 100,000 troops and 300 tanks charging
across the border into Kuwait. The royal family,
who had become convinced that Saddam was just
rattling his sabers, barely had time to escape the

country. Kuwait's army of 16,000 troops was no match for the invading force and was soundly defeated in just a few hours.

If Saddam thought the world would stand idly by and watch him annex a neighboring country, he was dead wrong. Within hours of the invasion a wave of outrage swept through the international community. In Washington, President George Herbert Walker Bush immediately clamped an embargo on Iraq, terminating the flow of goods to or from the country. Even more ominous for Saddam, at his command the aircraft carrier Independence set sail from its position in the Indian Ocean toward the Persian Gulf.

In what was by far the biggest in a long string of military blunders, Saddam had pitted himself against most of the civilized world and the reaction came swiftly. When a nervous Saudi Arabia, certain that it was next on Saddam's list, asked the United States for protection a few days after the attack, President Bush immediately ordered the deployment of troops to that country. In an address to Congress on September 11, President Bush praised our servicemen while warning Saddam that his attempt to crush Kuwait was doomed to failure:

"At this moment, our brave servicemen and women stand watch in that distant desert and on distant seas, side by side with the forces of more than 20 other nations. They are some of the finest men and women of the United States of America and they're doing one terrific job. These valiant Americans were ready at a moment's notice to leave their spouses and their children, to serve on the front line halfway around the world. They remind us who keeps America strong.

"Our objectives in the Persian Gulf are clear, our goals defined and familiar: Iraq must withdraw from Kuwait completely, immediately and without condition. Kuwait's legitimate government must be restored. The security and stability of the Persian Gulf must be assured. And American citizens abroad must be protected.

"Let me also make clear that the United States has no quarrel with the Iraqi people. Our quarrel is with Iraq's dictator and with his aggression. Iraq will not be permitted to annex Kuwait. That's not a threat, that's not a boast — that's just the way it's going to be."

With world opinion solidly against him and the full might of the U. S. military aimed squarely between his eyes, the Iraqi dictator realized he had painted himself into a corner. But backing down wasn't an option: Above all, being Saddam was about saving face and staying in power, so he launched a verbal offensive of his own against America and its allies. In a speech "to the Iraqi people, faithful Arabs and Muslims everywhere,"

Saddam appealed for an uprising against the allied coalition:

"We call on Arabs to do what they can within their means in light of God's laws and the sanctities of jihad and struggle against this infidel and occupying presence to expose, without hesitation and through all means, the actions of traitors and their allies of corruption and oppression.

"Those involved will be sorry and their gathering will be utterly routed if they undertake a military confrontation. Their footprints will be erased from the entire region and then Jerusalem will be restored, free and Arab, to the lap of faith and the faithful. Palestine will be liberated from the Zionist invaders and the Arab and Islamic nation will see a sun that will never set. They will be in God's protection when they have returned to the Almighty. God is great, God is great, God is great. Accursed be the lowly ones."

As it turned out, Saddam had grossly underestimated America's resolve. He was sure that the United States wouldn't bother to intervene in what he saw as an Arab matter, of no concern to foreigners, and he felt that American citizens wouldn't support a war on the opposite side of the world. He was wrong on both counts.

Early on the morning of Thursday, Jan. 17, 1991, air raid sirens began to blare in downtown Baghdad. Anti-aircraft batteries lit up the sky with a curtain of fire and suddenly one explosion after another shook the city as bombs and cruise missiles began to fall. In less than seven hours, more than 750 sorties were launched against targets in Iraq, including surface-to-air missile sites, command-and-control centers, air bases, communications installations and other military targets. Operation Desert Storm had begun.

Huddled in Baghdad's Al Rashid Hotel, news correspondents were, for the first time, able to show the aerial bombardment of an enemy live, in real time. Viewers watched in rapt amazement as Iraqi antiaircraft tracers peppered the sky, their popcorn explosions a lively counterpoint to the roar of allied jets overhead. As Tomahawk cruise missiles zigzagged toward their targets with pinpoint accuracy, Iraqi artillery fired blindly at the Air Force F-117 Nighthawk stealth fighters which had so easily penetrated their airspace.

Former CNN correspondent Peter Arnett later remembered it as a beautiful, starry night until the bombs began to fall. He and newsmen John Holliman and Bernard Shaw had a front-row seat at the window of their hotel room as the largest bombardment in history took place. Because the Iraqi government was still reeling with surprise at the sudden attack, there was no media censorship for the first few hours and the three men, who would later be known as the "Boys of Baghdad," were able to report freely on the attack via their CNN satellite link.

But the three were also in grave danger. Arnett recalled a bomb exploding just a few blocks away, sending a wave of heat through their window. As Bernard Shaw reported at the time, "It feels like the center of Hell." Throughout the long night, Iraqi security forces repeatedly tried to flush the men out of their hotel suite, and Shaw formulated a plan: If the Iraqis broke in, at least two of the newsmen would hide so they could continue reporting their eyewitness accounts.

When the sun rose the next morning, not a single allied aircraft had been lost despite the intense ground fire. Those few Iraqi aircraft that had managed to take off had fled to airfields in the northern part of the country. The presidential palace lay in ruins, as did the Ministry of Defense and the Baath Party headquarters. But an obstinate Saddam soon took to the airwaves, broadcasting his defiance on Iraqi state radio:

"O great Iraqi people, sons of our great people, valiant men of our courageous armed forces ... Satan's follower Bush committed his treacherous crime, he and the criminal Zionism. The great duel, the mother of all battles, between victorious right and the evil that will certainly be defeated has begun, God willing."

To rally Mideast support for his cause, Saddam

tried to present the war as a battle between Islam, the infidels of the West and the Zionists of Israel, but his imperialist actions had already spoken far louder than his empty words. The allied air campaign continued.

The day after the first allied attack, Saddam retaliated by launching a Scud missile at Israel. His plan was to goad the Israelis into striking back, which he hoped would gather support for him in the Arab world and weaken the international coalition President Bush had assembled.

The Scuds were already outdated technology by the time Saddam bought some 650 of them from the Russians, but they fit perfectly in the niche between his ground and air forces. In addition, they could be modified to carry chemical or biological agents, which gave him yet another threat to hold over his enemies.

The Scud is a direct descendant of the German V-2 rocket that terrorized London during the Blitz of World War II. Developed in Russia as the R-17 — and dubbed the SS-1 by NATO — the missile was designed to carry a 2,000-pound conventional warhead or a 100-kiloton nuclear device. First used in the 1973 Yom Kippur War, it has a range of 100 to 180 miles depending on its payload.

But that wasn't good enough for Saddam, who wanted a weapon capable of striking Israel. He put his scientists to work redesigning the Scud for longer range and the modified rocket they eventually came up with was named the al-Hussein, a hybrid that could be launched from a fixed site or from one of the mobile launchers his scientists had developed. The mobile units were supported by fuel trucks and supply vehicles designed to look like civilian buses and could be easily moved from place to place to evade allied air strikes.

The al-Hussein rocket had one nagging problem, however: The modifications Saddam had ordered tended to make it come apart in flight. Because the original Scud wasn't designed for the speed or range of the al-Hussein, missiles falling toward their targets at speeds faster than a bullet would often disintegrate into large chunks. Unfortunately, those multiple pieces could do more damage than a single rocket. On top of that, the more pieces there were, the harder it was for Patriot anti-missile batteries to intercept the warhead.

In *Desert Victory: The War for Kuwait*, author Norman Friedman noted that "Typically two missiles are fired at the target, but four would have to be fired at a broken-up Scud to insure that at least two attacked the warhead section. The fire unit's radars generally detected Scuds at about 70 miles and the unit engaged at 10-20 miles. Alerts were often provided by satellites originally launched to detect Soviet missiles and the time from alert to engagement was typically 6-7 minutes. The time from engagement to destruction of the missile was typically 15-18 seconds; the Patriots and the Scud closed at 2,000 to 4,000 feet per second."

The Patriot had been designed in the 1970s as an anti-aircraft missile, but in the 1980s it was retooled as an anti-missile weapon. The heart of the system is a computer-driven phased-array radar unit. The rocket is around 17 feet long and weighs 2,200 pounds, with a range of around 43 miles. It destroys its target by exploding nearby, slicing it to bits with shrapnel.

The Patriot drew first blood the day after the allied attack when Iraq fired a Scud at Saudi Arabia. A Patriot successfully intercepted the Scud, blowing it to bits. It was the first time that a missile had successfully destroyed another missile in the Gulf War.

By January 21, the United States had mounted more than 8,000 air sorties and had gained complete air superiority over Iraq, but Saddam's mobile Scud launchers were proving much more elusive than predicted. The Russian-built rockets continued to fall on Tel Aviv and Saudi Arabia, even though Patriot missiles managed to destroy many of them. But with some Scuds still getting through the Patriot defense shield, worries of chemical, biological or nerve gas attacks began to grow.

Fortunately, the Scuds were notoriously inaccurate. With no guidance whatsoever once they had left their launchers, they had only a 50 percent chance of landing within a mile of their target.

On January 22, Iraqi forces began to set fire to oil wells all over Kuwait, touching off an unprecedented environmental disaster. In addition, Saddam ordered that oil be dumped into the Persian Gulf to further distract the coalition. From January to May 1991, 11 million barrels of oil were poured into the Gulf's formerly pristine waters, coating more than 800 miles of Kuwaiti and Saudi Arabian coastline with a thick sludge, 20 times larger than the Alaskan oil spill caused by the *Exxon Valdez*.

Meanwhile, the U.S bombing campaign raged on, often led by the remarkable F-117A stealth fighter. Unlike most conventional combat aircraft, the F-117 was designed to fly deep into enemy territory alone, without the support aircraft that usually accompanied other fighters. The F-117 was so sophisticated that it needed just one pilot and in the Gulf War flew only at night to maximize the element of surprise. Because of its stealthy radar-absorbing design, the F-117 was virtually invisible on radar, so a stealth fighter attack seemed to come from nowhere. The first notice the Iraqi troops had that there was an F-117 in their neighborhood was a violent explosion.

The plane was a marvel of technology, with a state-of-the-art navigational system that could put it on target with amazing accuracy. Its computer-driven fire control system allowed the pilot to hand over much of the details of a bombing run to the plane's electronic systems, which could deliver laser-guided bombs to their targets with incredible precision.

Also taking part in the aerial war was a fleet of B-52 Stratofortress bombers, which dropped about 30 percent of all the munitions during the conflict. The heavy bomber was originally developed in the 1940s and entered service with the Strategic Air Command in 1954. It was heavily used in Vietnam to bomb Vietcong strongholds. The plane could carry up to 60,000 pounds of bombs and it unleashed them on Iraqi positions around the clock in the Gulf War. Although aged, the planes have been upgraded with modern weapons systems and are even capable of delivering laser-guided bombs with nearly the same accuracy as the F-117.

On January 26, several Iraqi warplanes landed in Iran to escape destruction by the coalition forces and were promptly seized by Saddam's longstanding enemies.

The next day the war's first major dogfight broke out, with U.S. F-15 Strike Eagles downing four Iraqi aircraft — three Soviet-built MiG-23 fighters and one French-built Mirage.

As the bombing campaign continued unabated, Saddam's military infrastructure disintegrated bit by bit. His four nuclear research reactors, suspected of creating weapons-grade plutonium, were bombed to rubble, and his chemical and biological factories were badly damaged. All over Iraq, bridges, roads, power stations and other targets were vaporized under the coalition's relentless air campaign. Many of Saddam's planes that hadn't been destroyed on the ground had been flown to Iran and were out of the war. But on radio and television, the stubborn dictator still insisted that Iraq was winning the conflict.

On January 29, the United States and the Soviet Union issued a joint communiqué to Saddam offering him a cease-fire if he made an "unequivocal commitment" to withdraw his forces from Kuwait. The tyrant responded the next day by launching what he called "a lightning strike into the kingdom of evil," sending thousands of troops and scores of battle tanks streaming from Kuwait into Saudi Arabia, where they captured the abandoned town of Khafji. American forces immediately moved to root them out, and suffered the first ground casualties of the war when 11 Marines were killed in fierce fighting.

Claiming victory even though Iraqi losses in the battle had been much higher, Saddam began to amass his troops along the Saudi border. American intelligence spotted a 10-mile-long column of troops and armored vehicles moving toward Saudi Arabia on February 1 and sent waves of fighters and bombers to intercept it. The allied air attack decimated the Iraqi forces and put a quick end to Saddam's invasion plans.

On February 4 another milestone was reached, when the battleship *Missouri* fired her cannon in anger for the first time since the Korean War, blasting Iraqi positions inside Kuwait from her anchor point in the Persian Gulf. On February 7 she was joined by the Wisconsin and the two ships' massive 16-inch guns teamed up to rain death on the occupying forces in Kuwait.

It was reported that by this stage of the war, Iraq had sustained more than 50,000 casualties in the Kuwaiti theater and had lost more than 1,110 artillery pieces and 800 armored personnel carriers. Most significantly, some 1,300 of Saddam's Soviet-made battle tanks had been destroyed or damaged.

Such extensive damages could be largely attributed to America's advanced technological superiority on all fronts. With no cover to hide behind in the vast expanses of the Kuwaiti desert, Saddam's tank commanders had taken to burying their vehicles in the sand to hide from air strikes. But the sun's infrared rays, which create heat, were able to penetrate deeply enough to significantly warm up the buried tanks. When night came and the desert rapidly cooled, the metal vehicles were slow to give up their stored heat and showed up as glowing targets on American infrared sensors. The tank commanders had the choice of staying underground to be obliterated or coming up to the surface where they were cannon fodder for aircraft like the A-10 Thunderbolt (affectionately known as the Warthog because of its blunt snout) whose armor-penetrating slugs would make short work of them.

With his war machine crumbling around him, Saddam decided to use a stalling tactic. He made an announcement stating he might be willing to withdraw from Kuwait, but put so many conditions on the move that it amounted to, as President Bush put it, "a cruel hoax." Included in Saddam's demands: the Israeli withdrawal from part of its lands, the recognition of Iraq's historical right to Kuwait and the retirement of Iraq's $40 billion foreign debt to that country. He also wanted the allies to foot the bill for the reconstruction of postwar Iraq.

Not surprisingly, these terms were immediately rejected. Instead, President Bush set a deadline for Saddam, saying that "the coalition will give Saddam Hussein until noon Saturday (February 23) to do what he must do — begin his immediate and unconditional withdrawal from Kuwait. We must hear publicly and authoritatively his accept-ance of these terms."

As usual, Saddam refused to back down. Instead, his troops set fire to even more Kuwaiti oil wells, blackening the sky over the besieged nation and creating vast oil lakes on the desert where no life could exist. It was the latest of Saddam's many bungled military decisions.

At 8 p.m. EST on February 23, thousands of allied soldiers under the command of General Norman Schwarzkopf rammed through Iraqi lines, storming across the border into Kuwait in the war's first large-scale ground assault. Terrified Iraqi soldiers surrendered by the thousands, with more than 20,000 giving up by the end of the sec-ond day of fighting. Those who couldn't locate an allied military outfit surrendered to TV camera crews. Coalition troops moved swiftly to encircle Saddam's Republican Guard units just north of the border.

The next day a force of more than 300 Black Hawk, Apache and Cobra attack helicopters and Chinook supply choppers launched a major air strike more than 50 miles into Iraq — the largest helicopter assault in history. The Chinooks airlifted troops and equipment of the 101st Airborne Division deep into Saddam's empire, taking the unprepared Iraqi forces by surprise and inducing a mass surrender.

When the 101st had secured its position, dubbed command base COBRA, it began moving north again. By nightfall it had seized control of Highway 8, a major conduit connecting Iraqi forces in Kuwait with Baghdad. By then many Iraqi forces had been cut off from their supply lines and coalition forces had succeeded in isolating many of Saddam's fighting units from each other. The noose was tightening.

The mechanized units leading the charge into Iraq sped forward at an unexpectedly rapid rate and began to outpace their supply vehicles. Many main battle tanks were capable of speeds of up to 50 miles an hour, while their supporting transports and fuel trucks could move at a rate of only 30 miles or so per hour. Commanders resorted to a leapfrog strategy, allowing the support vehicles to move out ahead of the main force, then allow the tanks to speed past them.

Thanks to technology, U.S. forces didn't have to stop at nightfall — Global Positioning System navigational equipment kept them continuously updated on their position, and advanced infrared night vision scopes and goggles combined with image-enhancement equipment made it easy to see what lay ahead. By midnight the first coalition forces had reached a position about 75 miles into Iraq.

To distinguish friend from foe and facilitate command and control of the huge force, a device called the Budd Light was attached to vehicle antennas. Invented by Henry C. "Budd" Croley of the Army Material Command, it consisted of infrared-emitting LEDs snapped onto the top of regular batteries. The purple lights were visible only through night-vision goggles and could be seen nearly a mile and a half away.

The U.S. 1st Infantry Division soon encountered one of Saddam's major lines of defense, built of high berms and crisscrossed by trenches of enemy soldiers. But the American tanks were fitted with plow blades and were able to smash right through the fortifications. Then combat earthmovers were brought in and, under covering fire from Bradley fighting vehicles, they filled in the trenches. Eventually 20 lanes were cut through the Iraqi positions and their neighboring minefields, and the coalition kept rolling.

While the Army neutralized Saddam's defenses, the Marines pushed farther into Kuwait toward the ultimate destination — Kuwait City. Before they could reach it, however, they had to contend with even more extensive Iraqi defenses, including not only berms and trenches but razor-sharp concertina wire and more dug-in enemy troops. As it turned out, however, the fierce battle that commanders had envisioned never materialized.

When the 1st Marine Division encountered the enemy and destroyed two Iraqi tanks in just a few minutes, Saddam's soldiers surrendered in droves. Altogether, the Marines gained 3,000 or so prisoners of war in the brief encounter.

As the Marines plowed ahead toward Kuwait City, they came across more earthworks and minefields and successfully cleared them all. They were also inundated with surrendering Iraqi troops, to the point where the huge number of captives became a logistical problem. By the end of the day, the Marines were 20 miles into Kuwait and had nearly 10,000 prisoners of war on their hands. But they knew it was no time for complacency: Saddam's Republican Guard was still ahead.

As the 3rd Armored Division pressed north on the allied left flank, they closed to within 40 miles of a large Iraqi force. Close air support strikes were called in, followed by helicopter attacks on the enemy positions. At around 15 miles, tactical missile batteries, artillery and rocket launchers further softened up Saddam's army as psychological operations teams broadcast a strong suggestion to the Iraqis that they surrender. The message did the trick: Only one attack was mounted by Iraq, and the 1st Armored Division responded by destroying around 50 enemy tanks in just 10 minutes.

On February 25, Iraqi forces attempted a coun-
terattack on allied positions at daybreak but they
were pushed back. Saddam's men continued
setting oil fires and 200 of them now blazed,
choking the sky with acrid black smoke. They also
continued launching Scud missiles into Israel and
Saudi Arabia. One hit a building in Dhahran
where American troops were stationed, killing 28
and wounding more than 100. It was the largest
one-day loss of life for the allies since the war
began.

On February 26, what became known as the
battle of 73 Easting erupted in the desert. The
name referred to a geographical line on military
maps and as American armored divisions
approached the spot they ran into a phalanx of
top-of-the-line Russian-built T-72 tanks. With
thermal imaging equipment, allied forces
destroyed one tank after another, but this time
there were no mass surrenders. The battle raged
for four hours and when the dust cleared the 2nd
Armored Cavalry had knocked out at least 29
tanks and 24 armored personnel carriers.

The Army's 2nd Armored Division Tiger Brigade
continued on toward a place called Mutla Ridge, all
of 25 feet above sea level but still the highest point
for hundreds of miles. On the way they destroyed
scores of enemy bunkers and took more than 1,600
prisoners. The ridge lay at an intersection of two

major highways and when it was taken, the Brigade could see one of the largest traffic jams in history, as hundreds of vehicles fleeing Kuwait lined up on nearby Highway 8.

When it was found that Iraqi troops and Republican Guard soldiers had commandeered civilian trucks and automobiles in their mad rush to escape from Kuwait, the Air Force and Navy were called in. The "Highway of Death" quickly became littered with burning and exploding trucks, cars and buses, while a steady stream of unsuspecting Iraqi soldiers raced out of Kuwait City in their stolen vehicles only to become engulfed in the carnage. The Tiger Brigade added its firepower and with shells, bombs and rockets decimating the column of vehicles, many of Saddam's men fled into the desert.

In their book *The Whirlwind War*, editors Frank Schubert and Theresa Kraus described the scene:

"Some drivers, seeing vehicles explode and burn, veered off the road in vain attempts to escape. Others stopped, dismounted and walked toward the Americans with raised hands. When the division staff detected elements of the Hammurabi Division of the Republican Guard moving across the 24th's front, General Barry McCaffrey concentrated the fire of nine artillery battalions and an Apache battalion on the once-elite enemy force. At dawn the next day, the 28th, hundreds of vehicles lay crumpled and smoking on Highway 8 and at scattered points across the desert."

When the ongoing dust storms finally cleared, those Iraqi soldiers still fighting could see a vast array of tanks, Bradley fighting vehicles and artillery pieces moving toward them — so many that the phalanx actually extended over the horizon. It was clear that the coalition was now firmly in control of the country. In just 90 hours, allied forces had destroyed an estimated 1,300 tanks, 1,200 infantry fighting vehicles and armored personnel carriers and 285 artillery pieces, while the number of captured enemy soldiers stood at more than 58,000. The next few hours saw the liberation of Kuwait City.

With the war's objective met, President Bush and his advisors decided to declare victory and call a cease-fire. With the conflict nearly 100 hours old, they set that symbolic point as the official end of the war. American forces could have easily taken Baghdad at that point, but there was a concern that the images of the "Highway of Death" could sour public opinion on the war and complicate the postwar political situation in the Mideast. President Bush took to the airwaves to make the official announcement, saying:

"Kuwait is liberated. Iraq's Army is defeated.

Our military objectives are met. It was a victory
for all the coalition nations, for the United
Nations, for all mankind and for the rule of law."

Saddam had been handed one of the most
crushing defeats in the history of warfare. Much
of his country lay in ruins and Iraq's economy,
already reeling from the Iran-Iraq war before his
invasion of Kuwait, was on the verge of collapse.
His army had sustained more than 150,000 casualties, thousands of his soldiers were prisoners of
war and his once-mighty army had been reduced
to a skeleton of its former self. As Lieutenant
General Tom Kelly put it: "Iraq went from the
fourth-largest army in the world to the second-
largest army in Iraq in 100 hours."

But Saddam wasn't about to admit defeat. In a
laughable postwar address to the people of Iraq,
the deluded dictator crowed: "You have won,
Iraqis. Iraq is the one who is victorious. Iraq has
succeeded in demolishing the aura of the United
States, the empire of evil, terror and aggression."

CHAPTER FOUR

SADDAM SURVIVES

The Gulf War — just another in a long list of military misfires instigated by Saddam — was a devastating blow to Iraq. It left the Iraqi military in tatters and cost the nation greatly in world public opinion. But what it didn't do was remove Saddam from power. Thus, overcome by his own egomania, Saddam considered himself and the nation of Iraq the victor.

This made perfect sense to Saddam, who had become a master of survival against overwhelming odds. Sure, thousands of Iraqi soldiers had been killed and huge amounts of equipment and material destroyed, but he was still standing and that, above all else, was the most important thing to him.

Indeed, the world had learned early in Saddam's bloody rule that there was no defeat where Saddam was concerned, no sign of weakness whatsoever, regardless of the truth or the effect his misguided hubris may have had on his nation and its economy. As long as Saddam was still alive and in charge, Iraq was a nation graced by God.

As proof to the world of his "victory" in the Gulf War, Saddam did not personally attend the ceremony with coalition military leaders on March 3, 1991, to sign the cease-fire and accept the United Nations' demands for Iraq's full withdrawal from Kuwait. Instead, he sent seven generals to endure that public humiliation. The private Saddam, however, was not above showing emotion — he reportedly wept like a baby in his mistress's arms at the sight of his once-mighty military lying in smoking ruins along the road to Kuwait.

However, Saddam's military strength had not been completely obliterated, as many initially believed. More than 20 divisions — as well as his air force — had been destroyed during the war, but four-and-a-half of Saddam's elite Republican Guard divisions had successfully fled Kuwait, surviving to fight another day.

In the years following the first Gulf War, many have questioned President George H.W. Bush's decision to stop in midstride the offensive that had the Iraqis on the run back in 1991. If given just a few more days, analysts said, coalition forces could have driven directly into Baghdad and literally knocked on Saddam's front door.

President Bush said he made his decision based on the best information he had at the time and he sticks to that decision even today. The goal of the war, he has repeatedly stated, was to remove Iraq from Kuwait, not create a regime change. Once that goal was achieved, it was time to go home.

"If we had tried to go in there and created more instability in Iraq, I think it would have been very bad for the neighborhood," the former president said during a speech at Tufts University. To have pursued Saddam and taken him out would have "instantly shattered" the delicate multinational coalition created for the war.

Secretly, however, it was hoped by many U.S. military officials that handing Saddam a humiliating defeat in Kuwait would compel the Iraqi military and/or an irate populace to take care of the problem on their own when they realized that their emperor had no clothes. But Saddam is nothing if not wily. He worked quickly and methodically to eliminate any hint of dissent within the military and the government, reward his most valuable allies and shore up his public standing through pompous speeches and public praise for defeating the Great Satan. Before the smoke had even cleared from the Iraqi desert, Saddam was standing tall and thumbing his nose at his enemies.

Not that there weren't a few hitches. On March

1, 1991, revolts broke out among the Shiites in southern Iraq. A few days later, there was an uprising among the Kurds in the north in response to a call by President Bush for "the Iraqi military and the Iraqi people to take matters into their own hands, to force Saddam the dictator to step aside." The situation looked so grim for Saddam that there were persistent rumors within the international community that the Iraqi strongman was seeking exile in Russia, a long-time ally of Iraq, or possibly India.

Sadly, both revolts were doomed from the start. Colin Powell, who was then Chairman of the Joint Chiefs of Staff, admitted in his memoirs: "Neither revolt had a chance. Nor, frankly, was their success a goal of our policy ... Our practical intention was to leave Baghdad enough power to survive as a threat to an Iran that remained bitterly hostile toward the United States."

Saddam moved quickly to stop the revolts before they could spread and seriously endanger his regime. The action was one of the most brutal and vicious assaults a head of state had ever authorized against his own people.

On March 6, 1991, two Republican Guard divisions under the command of Ali Hassan al-Majid flew into Basra and other Shiite strongholds aboard heavily armed helicopter gunships and massacred thousands of rebels. Within two weeks, the southern rebellion was completely quashed.

Saddam then sent in the Hammurabi division of the Republican Guard to eliminate Kurdish rebels to the north. Considered traitors by Saddam, the poorly equipped guerrillas fought valiantly but were no match for Saddam's military firepower. By the end of March, more than 20,000 Kurdish warriors had been massacred and their cities destroyed.

However, in his ruthless quest to maintain his grip on power, Saddam created a public relations nightmare that turned the entire world against him. Television images of the massacre's deadly aftermath only bolstered international outrage against Saddam and his blood-soaked regime. On April 5, 1991, the United Nations passed Resolution 688, which condemned "the repression of the Iraqi civilian population in many parts of Iraq" and demanded that the government allow humanitarian aid to reach Kurdish refugees.

Saddam loathed to do so, but he was in no position to deny the U.N. demand. On April 16, 20,000 American troops were sent to northern Iraq as part of Operation Provide Comfort. Under their protection, more than a million Kurds were allowed to return to their homeland and set up a fairly autonomous mini-state within Iraq.

To prevent further incidents of bloody ethnic

cleansing, the United States, Britain and France established no-fly zones in southern and northern Iraq. Enforced by frequent coalition fly-overs, the zones were off limits to Iraqi planes and helicopters and proved to be a thorn in Saddam's side for more than a decade.

Two days before passing Resolution 688, the United Nations passed another resolution to establish a special commission known as UNSCOM. It's mission was to "carry out immediate on-site inspection of Iraq's biological, chemical and missile capabilities, based on Iraq's declarations and the designation of any additional locations by the Special Commission itself."

Saddam could barely contain his rage at the indignities heaped upon his country by the United Nations and, specifically, the United States. Unwilling from the very beginning to cooperate with the United Nations directive, Saddam began a campaign of stonewalling, deceit and treachery that continued for almost a dozen years — until President George W. Bush said "Enough!" and set out to finish the job his father had started.

The disarmament of Iraq was supposed to take less than six months, but that was assuming Saddam would cooperate. He didn't. First, he told the United Nations that all of Iraq's Scud missiles had been destroyed during the Gulf War. When that was quickly proved to be a lie, Saddam backpedaled and admitted to possessing 52 of the deadly missiles, as well as 1,000 tons of chemical weapons. However, he denied that Iraq had biological weapons or any desire to acquire nuclear weapons. Iraq's developing nuclear program, he said, was strictly peaceful.

But as inspectors from the United Nations and the International Atomic Energy Agency started to dig deeper, they learned that Saddam's weapons of mass destruction programs were far larger than anyone had suspected. They also learned that a tremendous amount of weapons technology had survived the war.

In short, Saddam may have lost the Gulf War, but he still remained an extremely dangerous and unpredictable threat to the entire world.

Just two months into their inspections, UNSCOM and IAEA inspectors located nearly 20 kilograms of enriched uranium — and the equipment to make more. A peaceful nuclear program? Apparently not. This was the stuff from which nuclear weapons were made. Saddam had not yet achieved his goal of possessing atomic weapons, but it was clear he was making every effort to do so.

Additional proof came from an Iraqi scientist who defected during the Gulf War. He told American officials that the Saddam regime had been actively trying to make weapons-grade uranium and that four secret installations had survived the allied attack.

As the weeks and months passed, evidence of Saddam's lies piled up:

- When IAEA inspectors tried to enter a secret nuclear facility, armed guards barred the door and fired into the air.
- August 1991, U.N. inspectors discovered yet another prohibited weapon not initially declared by Saddam — a "super gun" capable of inflicting tremendous damage.
- Weapons inspectors confirmed that Saddam possessed four times the amount of chemical weapons that he had declared.

Saddam's stonewalling and lies angered the U.N. Security Council, which repeatedly demanded that he abide by the rules of the cease-fire his nation had signed. However, Saddam was too arrogant for that, nitpicking the agreement and offering halfhearted, partial compliance only when backed against the wall by international criticism or the threat of military action.

Saddam often cried that he was the victim of a U.S.-led international conspiracy against Iraq, but few listened. The United States took the lead in demanding that Saddam hold to his word, stating repeatedly that neither weapons inspections nor economic sanctions would be lifted until Saddam revealed the truth about his programs for weapons of mass destruction.

However, Iraq's military capability was only a small part of the problem. The bigger concern was Saddam himself and the powerful grip he maintained in Baghdad. "Iraqis will be made to pay the price while Saddam Hussein is in power," noted Robert Gates, President Bush's national security advisor. "Any easing of sanctions will be considered only when there is a new government."

In an effort to make that happen, the United States started sending financial support to the Iraqi National Congress, a vocal opponent of the Saddam regime, in the hope that its members would help topple the Iraqi government. At the same time, the CIA became involved in efforts to trigger a military coup. However, neither effort proved effective.

Weapons inspections continued for the next couple of years, though Saddam became increasingly unwilling to cooperate. Finally, in January 1993, the U.S. Security Council declared that Iraq was in "material breach" of the cease-fire.

If Saddam wouldn't cooperate willingly, the United States, Britain and France vowed to take out his weapons of mass destruction programs by force. On January 18, with just two days remaining in President Bush's presidency, 45 cruise missiles were launched at a manufacturing complex connected to Iraq's nuclear program.

Saddam was livid at the attack and vowed revenge against President Bush. The conflict between the two leaders became deeply personal when Saddam authorized the assassination of the former president during a well-publicized visit to Kuwait. American intelligence was well aware of the plot and the elder Bush was never in serious danger, but the United States couldn't let such a flagrant act go unchallenged. On President Bill Clinton's authorization, 23 cruise missiles rained down on Iraq's intelligence headquarters, blowing it to bits.

But Saddam was never one to learn lessons easily. In 1994, he tried to bully his way out of his international obligations by amassing his fabled Republican Guard at the Kuwaiti border. His threat was clear: Leave me alone or face another war. The international community was outraged and thousands of U.S. troops, supported by the British and French, lined up to face Saddam's troops eyeball to eyeball. Like most bullies, Saddam was a coward at heart and he quickly backed down rather than face another humiliating defeat.

A year later, things got even worse for Saddam when his son-in-law defected to Jordan and reported that the Iraqi leader had been hiding a massive nuclear weapons program. "We were ordered to hide everything from the beginning," Hussein Kamel said in an interview.

Saddam responded by saying that it was Kamel's idea to hide the program. As proof, U.N. inspectors were taken to Kamel's farm, where they found reams of information about Iraq's weapons of mass destruction programs. But rather than placate an angry world, the information only further proved that Iraq was in possession of or still pursuing weapons of mass destruction in direct violation of the U.N. resolution.

Faced with the prospect of more crippling sanctions, Saddam grudgingly agreed to a program in which money from the sale of Iraqi oil would be used to pay for food and other humanitarian aid for the Iraqi people. But Saddam managed to corrupt even that philanthropic endeavor, pumping huge amounts of extra oil on the side and secretly selling it to Syria, Jordan and Turkey. Saddam then used the money from this massive smuggling scheme — estimated at between $2 billion to 3 billion a year — to fund his luxurious lifestyle, reward his supporters and rebuild his beleaguered military.

Indeed, Saddam amassed a personal fortune by skimming money from Iraq's oil exports while many of his own people lived in abject poverty. Following the Gulf War, the government of

Kuwait asked internationally renowned private
investigator Jules Kroll to determine the extent of
Saddam's hidden wealth and locate assets that
Kuwait could claim for war reparations. Using
information provided by Iraqi defectors, intelligence agencies and corporate records, Kroll and
his associates determined that Saddam's multi-
billion-dollar secret financial network was run by
his half brother, Barzan al-Tikriti, and his son-in-
law, Hussein Kamel. "This is an organized crime
activity and it's been going on for a long time,"
Kroll said in 1991. "You've got basically one
family. I mean, this is the equivalent of the
Gambino family."

Kroll's report was given to the U.S. Treasury's
Office of Foreign Assets Control, which hit
Saddam hard in the wallet by seizing $2.4 billion
in cash, real estate and other holdings. These
assets remain frozen today, though the seizure
did little to impact Saddam's personal wealth.
"He's had plenty of time to rebuild it," Kroll said
in an interview. "He's had a lot of organizations
that have been willing to do business with him in
terms of smuggling and doing business through
front companies. I think it was a temporary
disruption."

As Saddam continued his policy of delay and
harass, U.N. weapons inspectors found their job
increasingly difficult. They were frequently brow-

beaten by Iraqi officials, denied access to strategic facilities and once even had a rocket-propelled grenade fired at their headquarters. Worst of all, though, a tired United Nations gradually took all the teeth out of the inspection effort by agreeing to Iraqi-imposed restrictions on where inspectors could go. Included in buildings listed as off-limits were Saddam's presidential palaces — huge, ornate structures that covered nearly 38 square miles of land. Iraqi officials also tried to have Americans removed from the inspection teams, claiming some of them were spies working for the CIA.

Pushed to the limit by Saddam's refusal to abide by U.N. demands and his obvious insistence on pursuing weapons of mass destruction, U.S. officials took a different tack — rather than wasting time playing games with Saddam, they set their sights on a complete regime change. In September 1997, Congress passed the Iraq Liberation Act, which stated: "It should be the policy of the United States to support efforts to remove the regime headed by Saddam Hussein from power in Iraq and promote the emergence of a democratic government to replace that regime." Nearly $100 million was budgeted to force Saddam from power.

Three months after the Iraq Liberation Act was passed, UNSCOM head Richard Butler officially pulled his teams out of Iraq. Saddam's complete refusal to cooperate, coupled with escalating harassment, made it nearly impossible for the teams to do their jobs, Butler said.

The inspection teams may have made a dent in Saddam's weapons of mass destruction programs, but they had not destroyed them. In their final report, inspectors said that Iraq had not accounted for 360 tons of chemical warfare agents — including 1.5 tons of deadly VX nerve agent. Also still missing was up to 3,000 tons of compounds used in the manufacture of chemical weapons; special growth media for the manufacture of biological agents, including anthrax, and more than 30,000 special munitions for the delivery of chemical and biological agents.

Saddam remained the mad dog loose in the global community, a deadly menace to all around him. Outlining U.S. policy on the matter, President Bill Clinton said, "So long as Saddam remains in power he will remain a threat to his people, his region and the world. With our allies, we must pursue a strategy to contain him and to constrain his weapons of mass destruction program, while working toward the day Iraq has a government willing to live in peace with its people and with its neighbors."

These were strong words, but they carried no real bite. President Clinton had no desire to go to war again with Iraq because at that point the United States stood practically alone in opposition to the Saddam regime. In fact, mirroring current events, the only country also willing to take a stand against Iraq was Britain. France had adopted a much softer stance because it hoped to obtain some of the lucrative contracts to rebuild Iraq's ravaged oil and gas industry, and Russia was willing to mollycoddle the Butcher of Baghdad in hopes of recovering some of the $20 billion debt owed by Iraq.

President Clinton, figuring he had more to gain by working for peace between the Arabs and the Israelis, put Iraq on the back burner. This greatly chagrined many political conservatives, who lobbied the president via letter to publicly support a coup against Saddam, station troops in the region to move against Baghdad when the time was right and to recognize an Iraqi government in exile. Those signing the letter included Donald Rumsfeld, Richard Perle and Paul Wolfowitz — future architects of President George W. Bush's policy toward Saddam and Iraq.

George W. Bush campaigned on a foreign policy that pretty much mimicked his father's position on Iraq, saying he would try to rebuild an international coalition against Saddam's regime and push to ensure that Saddam lived up to the agreement his country had signed at the end of the Gulf war.

However, President Bush's position on Iraq changed quickly and dramatically when the al Qaeda network, headed by Osama bin Laden, brought international terrorism to American soil for the very first time. Its attacks on the World Trade Center and the Pentagon on September 11, 2001, stunned the American public, which had long believed that terrorism was something that only affected other countries. Initial fear was quickly replaced by outrage, which gave way to a demand for retribution. Those who had attacked America had to pay.

But the terror wasn't over yet. Just a month after the attack on the World Trade Center and the Pentagon, another attack took place, this time in South Florida. Only the weapon wasn't a hijacked airplane, it was bacteria. Specifically a bacterium called anthrax.

The first victim of the first bioterrorism attack in the United States was Bob Stevens, a 63-year-old photo editor for *The Sun* tabloid. Stevens had fallen ill while visiting his daughter in North Carolina, but had felt well enough to drive back home. Just hours after his arrival, he became delirious and was racked with fever. His wife Maureen rushed him to the hospital, where the initial diagnosis was spinal meningitis. By the time it was learned that Stevens' illness was really inhalation anthrax, it was too late. He died the next day.

The news sent shockwaves throughout the United States. Anthrax was a known killer — and a particularly effective biological weapon — but it had affected only 18 Americans in the entire 20th century. It was quickly determined that Stevens had not been exposed to the deadly bacteria naturally, as occasionally happens. Someone had sent a letter full of the deadly germs to his workplace with intent to kill. Shortly after Stevens' death, anthrax-covered letters began showing up nationwide — including the U.S. Senate building addressed to Tom Daschle and Patrick Leahy, and the offices of NBC News. Spores had also leaked from the letters, contaminating mail facilities. By the end of the crisis, five people — including a 94-year-old Connecticut woman — were dead. As of this writing, the terrorist behind the letters has not been caught.

President Bush was more than eager to give the American people the revenge they so desperately wanted and deserved. In the wake of the September 11 attacks he sent troops into Afghanistan — for years an al Qaeda stronghold — to remove the anti-American Taliban government and locate terrorist leader Osama bin Laden. His message was crystal clear: Any nation harboring terrorists would be considered an enemy of the United States.

Though there was no immediate evidence that

Saddam was directly involved in the September 11 attacks, President Bush was certain the dictator had played a covert role, most likely by making Iraq available as a training center and haven for terrorist groups. It made sense, considering Saddam's years-long hatred of the United States and his desperate search for weapons of mass destruction — weapons that, if acquired, would almost certainly be used against the United States and its international interests.

Without revealing the president's initial suspicions, the Bush administration let it be known shortly after the September 11 attacks that Saddam was not only on their radar but practically in their crosshairs. Stopping terrorism "... is not simply a matter of capturing people and holding them accountable, but removing sanctuaries, removing the support systems, ending states that sponsor terrorism," warned Deputy Secretary of Defense Paul Wolfowitz.

Within hours of the terrorist attacks, Secretary of State Donald Rumsfeld told his aides to come up with plans to hit hard at Iraq. Intelligence information gathered shortly after the attack suggested a possible Iraqi link to Osama bin Laden and Secretary Rumsfeld saw the opportunity to take out Saddam as well. He ordered the military to immediately begin working on strike plans and ordered that all available information on any possible link between Saddam and al Qaeda be brought to his attention. "Go massive," Secretary Rumsfeld instructed. "Sweep it all up." At that moment, Saddam, along with Osama bin Laden, had become an enemy marked for eradication.

In the White House, President Bush quickly and decisively formulated his policy toward Saddam. Bolstered by a cadre of no-nonsense Republican conservatives such as Deputy Secretary Wolfowitz and Vice President Dick Cheney, the president decided from the very beginning that there would be no more game-playing where Saddam was concerned. The Butcher of Baghdad would be ousted — period. Whether he left peacefully or facing the muzzle of a gun was his choice, but one way or the other, his blood-regime was going to end.

Behind closed doors, the hawks in Bush's cabinet acknowledged that the September 11 terrorist attacks had demonstrated America's vulnerability. Despite efforts to bolster security nationwide, the United States simply couldn't take the risk of its greatest enemies one day procuring the kinds of weapons of mass destruction that would make the events of September 11 look minor by comparison. Rather than contain Saddam, the only way to be sure he wouldn't plunge a knife into the heart of America was to remove him from the equation.

In the days following September 11, President

Bush seemed like a changed man. Caught off-balance by the terrorist attacks, he quickly regained his footing and vowed immediately that such a thing would never, ever happen again on American soil. In the eyes of many, the president's resolve had taken on an almost religious fervor. Protecting the United States had become his primary concern and guaranteeing that protection meant eliminating Saddam. If the rest of the world was with him, great. If not, the United States would do the job alone.

Not everyone in the president's administration agreed with that position. One of the most vocal opponents was Secretary of State Colin Powell, the commander of American forces during the first Gulf War. A cautious and thoughtful man, Secretary Powell felt that the president was taking a great risk by having the United States go gunning for Saddam by itself. He preferred a coalition led by the United States and supported by its allies. But as history revealed, America's allies — specifically France and Germany — turned a deaf ear to suggestions that Saddam be taken out sooner rather than later. In the end, only the United States and Britain stood shoulder-to-shoulder against the Iraqi dictator, though more than 30 nations offered positional support.

U.S. pressure against Iraq built steadily through 2002. In January, President Bush let the world know exactly where he stood during his State of the Union Address in which he called Iraq, Iran and North Korea an "axis of evil" because of their ongoing pursuit of weapons of mass destruction.

Meanwhile, U.S. intelligence continued to gather evidence linking Saddam and the al Qaeda terrorist network. There was little direct proof, but a lot of small pieces, when combined, helped build the president's case. The Bush team also pressed the issue of Saddam's quest for weapons of mass destruction in general and nuclear weapons in particular. It was unwise for the United States to sit idly by until one of its most vociferous enemies either constructed or purchased a nuclear weapon, the president said. It wasn't a matter of if, it was a matter of when — and that day could never be allowed to come. Though the United States had never done so before, the smartest move, the move that absolutely guaranteed America's safety, was pre-emptive action against this known aggressor.

The future of the United States was on President Bush's mind when the decision was made — a perilous future if he didn't act. "I don't want history to look back and say, 'Where was President Bush?' " he explained. " 'How come he didn't act on behalf of the security of the American people?' "

In March, it has been reported, President Bush

was walking by the office of National Security Advisor Condoleezza Rice when he overheard her talking with three Senators on how best to deal with Saddam through the United Nations. Sticking his head in the door, the president smiled and said, "F*** Saddam. We're taking him out."

In typical Texas style, President Bush had thrown down a gauntlet that couldn't be ignored. One way or another, he vowed, he would do what his father had stopped short of doing 11 years before. He would take out Saddam Hussein.

The modest home in Tikrit, north of Baghdad, where Saddam Hussein was born. The boy was savagely beaten by his stepfather, introducing him to the violence that would mark his life.

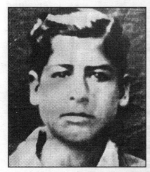

Hussein at the age of 16 (above left) and 21 (above right). His attempt to assassinate president Abdul Karim Qassem by blocking his motorcade ended in failure (right).

The future president at the age of 23 (left) in Cairo, Egypt, and with friends in Syria (below) during his four-year exile. Despite initially failing to shoot his way into power, Hussein was determined to return to Iraq.

As vice president of the Iraqi Revolutionary Command Council, Hussein meets with French president George Pompidou (above) and future French president Jacques Chirac (below). The French proved to be outspoken opponents against the U.S. efforts to remove the Iraqi dictator from power in 2003.

The Iraqi vice president visits the president of Cuba,
Fidel Castro, in 1978. Both countries hostile politics
toward the United States made them natural allies.

On July 16, 1979, Hussein was sworn in as the Iraqi president (above). The dictator enjoys a Cuban cigar (right) - a gift from his friend Fidel Castro.

Saddam welcomes Palestinian Liberation Organization Chairman Yasser Arafat to his country in 1980. The two leaders shared a passion for terror.

Saddam Hussein seated with his wife and one of his daughters in a family portrait. His sons Uday and Qusay (right) proved to be as bloodthirsty as their father. His two sons-in-law (left) were murdered after defecting to Jordan.

The Reverend Jesse Jackson visited Hussein in 1990, hoping to end the long-running Iran-Iraq war that left an estimated 1.4 million killed or wounded.

Undeterred after an unsuccessful invasion of Kuwait and the Persian Gulf War in 1991, the trigger-happy tyrant fires a rifle into the air during a military parade.

The president flanked by his sons Uday (left) and Quasay (right). Speaking out against Saddam or his sons was tantamount to a death sentence.

After receiving 100 percent of the votes from the Iraqi Revolutionary Council to win re-election, the president celebrates by brandishing a sword.

Outspokenly defiant to the end, Hussein grants a televised interview in February 2003.

Saddam leads a military strategy session after ignoring a U.S. ultimatum to leave Iraq.

Hussein speaks with members of his elite Republican Guard prior to the U.S.-led Operation Iraqi Freedom. In the face of unrelenting aerial bombing and a crushing ground assault, Iraqi resistance quickly collapsed.

Baghdad burns after an air raid by U.S. forces. The presidential palaces and other strategic sites were targeted to minimize civilian casualties.

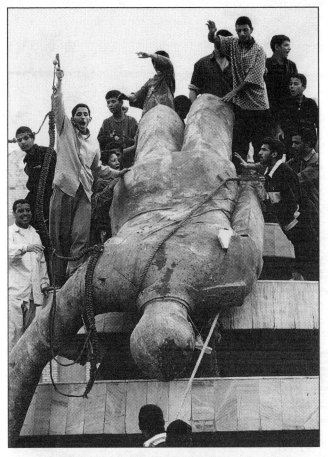

*Iraqi citizens celebrate their liberation atop a
destroyed statue of their former oppressor.
U.S. forces were warmly welcomed with singing
and dancing after their quick victory.*

U.S. Marine Corporal Edward Chin of New York drapes the stars and stripes over the face of a statue of Saddam Hussein in Baghdad.

Having won the capital, U.S. tanks occupy the driveway of one of the presidential palaces.

*American soldiers enjoy their victory in style –
relaxing in a lavish presidential palace formerly
occupied by the Butcher of Baghdad.*

Iraqi firemen attempt to douse the remains of a building thought to be Saddam's hideout. A lightning strike by a B-1 bomber reduced it to a smoldering crater.

CHAPTER FIVE

TARGET: SADDAM

President George W. Bush was adamant about removing Saddam Hussein from power as quickly as possible, and both he and his advisors knew that military action would probably be the only way to do it.

However, the international climate was quite different from when his father had confronted Saddam more than a decade earlier. Back then, the evil dictator had invaded a neighboring nation, an unprovoked act of war that rallied the world around the U.S.-led coalition formed to drive Saddam's army back across the border.

When the younger Bush decided to go after Saddam following the September 11 attacks, things were less black and white. Despite strong suspicions and suggestive bits of intelligence information, there was no smoking gun that conclusively proved

Iraq was in league with Osama bin Laden's al Qaeda network. And though Saddam was definitely on a quest for bigger and better weapons of mass destruction, his only acts of aggression were the atrocities his regime inflicted on its own people — and that had been going on for decades.

In an effort to strengthen U.S. credibility within the international community, Secretary of State Colin Powell persisted in encouraging the president to build a solid coalition of world leaders and seek a U.N. resolution approving military action against Iraq should Saddam fail to disarm. "It's nice to say you can do it unilaterally, except you can't," Secretary Powell told the president, adding that unilateral action conceivably could tear apart everything else the United States had accomplished — and hoped to accomplish — in the Middle East.

Secretary Powell was practically alone within the Bush Cabinet regarding the issue. Vice President Dick Cheney, Secretary of Defense Donald Rumsfeld and many others felt that going through the United Nations and trying to get backing from American allies would ultimately prove a costly waste of time and play further into Saddam's strategy of diplomatic stonewalling. "A return of (weapons) inspectors would prove no assurance whatsoever of (Saddam's) compliance with U.N. resolutions," Vice President Cheney noted.

Nonetheless, President Bush finally gave in to Secretary Powell's pleas and on September 12 — significant in that it was exactly a year and a day after the terrorist attacks in New York and Washington — he took his case before the United Nations.

Speaking before the U.N. General Assembly, President Bush methodically outlined why Saddam was a threat not only to the United States but the entire world. The president chose not to focus on what Saddam might do — a "what if" game that made many world leaders uncomfortable when it came to military action. Instead, he detailed point by point what Saddam had done in the past to prove he could not be trusted.

It was a long litany of broken promises, falsehoods and downright deceit. The president noted, for example, that Saddam had violated virtually every agreement he made when he secured a cease-fire with coalition forces at the end of the first Gulf War. One of the most important of the agreements — all of which had been approved in resolutions by the U.N. Security Council — was a pledge by Saddam to stop manufacturing weapons of mass destruction, destroy those he already had and allow an international team of inspectors to monitor and verify his compliance.

Of course, Saddam never did any of those things. Like Hitler, he had become a master at tricking the world by signing international agreements he had absolutely no intention of honoring. "To suspend hostilities and spare himself, Iraq's dictator accepted a series of commitments," a grim-faced President Bush told the United Nations. "The terms were clear: to him and to all. And he agreed to prove he is complying with every one of those obligations. He has proven instead only his contempt for the United Nations, and for all his pledges. By breaking every pledge — by his deceptions and his cruelties — Saddam Hussein has made the case against himself."

The president would have preferred to immediately begin military action against a threatening foe the world knew could never be trusted, but he held back. To maintain peace, the president said, Iraq would have to meet the following demands:

- Immediately and unconditionally foreswear, disclose and remove or destroy all weapons of mass destruction, long-range missiles and all related material.
- End all support for terrorism and act to suppress it.
- Cease persecution of Iraq's civilian population, including Shiites, Sunni, Kurds and Turkomans.
- Release or account for all Gulf War personnel whose fate is still unknown.
- Immediately end all illicit trade outside the oil-for-food program.

If Iraq met all of these conditions, President Bush said, it would signal a new openness and accountability in Iraq and make way for the prospect of a government based on respect for human rights, economic liberty and internationally supervised elections.

One can only picture Saddam chuckling to himself as the president listed one by one the demands the dictator would have to meet to avoid military action. To honor even one of them would have been a sign of humiliating weakness in Saddam's cruel eyes and an indication to the entire world that he was willing to lie down with the American infidels — his most hated enemy.

It was obvious to all that President Bush's demands were a peaceful effort to tear down the very framework of the Saddam regime, a noble but futile endeavor. Saddam had broken every agreement he had ever signed. Why would he start doing the right thing now?

President Bush knew from the beginning that Saddam would never honor the demands. In fact, he was counting on it. Saddam may have smiled and agreed, but his deceitful betrayal of those agreements was inevitable — and when he backtracked, the president would have the additional evidence he needed to justify the dictator's immediate removal.

The unspoken message in President Bush's

speech before the United Nations was that if —
or more likely when — Saddam failed to comply,
the United States was prepared to take immediate military action. The United Nations must
enforce the resolutions it passes, the president
stated, or risk becoming irrelevant.

"If Iraq's regime defies us again, the world must
move deliberately, decisively to hold Iraq to
account," President Bush said. "We will work with
the U.N. Security Council for the necessary resolutions. But the purposes of the United States
should not be doubted.

"The Security Council resolutions will be
enforced — the just demands of peace and security will be met — or action will be unavoidable.
And a regime that has lost its legitimacy will also
lose its power."

Iraq reacted immediately to President Bush's
speech. The very next day, in Baghdad, Deputy
Prime Minister Tariq Aziz condemned the president's comments and said the speech was "full of
lies." However, just four days later, in an apparent
attempt to gain international confidence, Iraqi
officials said that weapons inspectors could return
"without conditions." Officials in France, Russia,
China and many Arab nations felt the offer was
sufficient to hold off stronger action for the present, but President Bush was unimpressed. The
offer, he said, was nothing but a ploy.

Even as the U.N. Security Council began the arduous task of hammering out a resolution that would force Saddam to end his evil ways, President Bush worked on garnering the support he would need to take military action against Iraq when the inevitable time arrived. He was under no illusion that Saddam would disarm and cease committing atrocities against his own people — in short, commit political suicide by weakening his own regime — and he believed it was imperative that he get his own political and military ducks in a row.

On September 19, the president sent to Congress a resolution that would authorize him to use "all means determined to be appropriate, including force" to defend the United States against the ongoing threat posed by Iraq. Ordinarily Congress must declare war, but this was different, the president explained. While the United States had not been directly attacked by Iraq, the threat was growing every day and action had to be taken. A resolution by Congress giving him the authorization to act at his discretion would simplify matters greatly.

The day after President Bush sent his proposed resolution to Congress, the White House released a new strategic doctrine that endorsed preemptive action against any nation that posed a serious threat to the United States.

The concept of pre-emptive action on the part of the United States was foreign to most people. In the past, this nation responded only to overt aggression, such as the Japanese attack on Pearl Harbor that brought America into World War II. But times had changed, White House officials explained. A nation didn't have to directly attack the United States to pose a threat to its security — all it had to do was aid and train terrorists such as those who flew the jets into the World Trade Center and the Pentagon.

We were facing an insidious new enemy, the White House warned — an enemy that threatened the safety and security of the United States through covert acts of terrorism rather than overt, declared aggression. Nations that actively supported anti-American terrorists were by definition an enemy of the state and thus potential targets of preemptive action.

On September 26, Secretary Rumsfeld revealed that there was evidence that al Qaeda terrorists had recently been in Baghdad and that the terrorist organization had requested Saddam's help in acquiring weapons of mass destruction. Other nations challenged the information, but the White House held firm, saying that the classified evidence was still more proof that Saddam was in league with anti-American forces.

Hans Blix, the chief U.N. weapons inspector,

reported on October 1 that Iraq had finally agreed to terms for inspections, but that eight presidential sites were still off limits. The qualification only proved to the world that Saddam was still up to his old tricks. After all, Iraq had declared earlier that weapons inspectors were welcome to return "without restrictions." With the clock ticking, U.N. and Iraqi negotiators returned to the table to hammer out another draft of the inspections agreement.

In an interview the next day, Secretary Powell offered a slightly softer American position on the Iraq issue, noting that the president's policy of regime change could leave Saddam in power if he fully disarmed and allowed U.N. weapons inspectors to verify it. This requested much more of Saddam than anyone thought he'd accept, but it helped the White House placate world leaders who felt the Bush administration was pushing too hard for military action.

A week later, President Bush went on television to ask members of Congress to back him on Iraq. Approval of the resolution didn't mean war was inevitable, the president said, but it was important that the United States let Iraq and the rest of the world know that it would respond to all threats quickly and forcefully. On October 10, the House of Representatives approved the president's resolution authorizing the use of force against Iraq by a vote of 296-133. The Senate granted its approval the next day with a vote of 77-23.

When terrorists blew up a night club in Bali on October 12 killing 187 people — including several Australian and American tourists — the need for the resolution seemed justified. Days later, the president suggested that the attack might be linked to Iraq.

On October 15, Saddam won another presidential referendum with almost 100 percent of the vote. The outcome of the so-called election, which granted Saddam another seven years as president, was no surprise because the ruthless dictator had run unopposed. The event was the topic of jokes worldwide and served as additional proof that Saddam still maintained an iron grip on his country.

In November, after weeks of struggle and backroom negotiating, the U.N. Security Council unanimously passed a resolution declaring Iraq in "material breach" of earlier U.N. resolutions and demanding that Saddam reveal everything about his weapons of mass destruction programs or face "serious consequences." The resolution required renewed weapons inspections and provided a detailed schedule for them.

The resolution sounded good in theory, but it quickly became apparent that the U.N. Security

Council wasn't particularly eager to follow through. Only the United States, Britain and Bulgaria felt that Iraq posed a serious and ongoing threat. The remaining members of the body, many of whom had vested economic interests in Iraq, seemed satisfied to slap Saddam on the wrist and let him continue his evil ways.

His regime uncomfortably in the spotlight, Saddam grudgingly accepted the U.N. resolution on November 13 and a U.N. advance team arrived in Baghdad five days later to begin weapons inspections. The program began in earnest on November 27 — the first U.N. inspections since 1998.

Weapons inspections sounded good in theory, but it quickly became apparent that Saddam was still playing the same games. Though he'd offered unconditional access, inspectors found themselves facing many of the same obstacles they had confronted earlier, including passive-aggressive noncompliance on the part of Iraqi officials. Like children being punished, they did only as much as they needed to avoid getting into trouble and made things as difficult as possible for the inspectors.

The inspectors soon admitted that it could take several months for them to search every site in Iraq. This did not sit well with the president, who was eager to see a quick regime change within the rogue state. Saddam's charade had gone on long enough, and it was time for decisive action.

The president quickly let everyone know that should weapons inspections fail, the United States was prepared to step in and take care of Saddam itself, regardless of how the U.N. Security Council felt about it. "Saddam Hussein is a threat to our nation," the president explained during a press conference. "September 11 changed the strategic thinking, at least as far as I was concerned, for how to protect our country ... I think the threat is real (and) I'm confident the American people understand that when it comes to our security, if we need to act, we will act and we really don't need United Nations approval to do so."

By November, the U.S. military was already months into preparation for an attack on Iraq. In fact, Gen. Tommy Franks, the commander in the Persian Gulf, had delivered a preliminary invasion plan to the White House two days before the president first addressed the U.N. Security Council. As military action grew increasingly likely, President Bush eagerly outlined his plan to democratize Iraq once Saddam was gone. The Saddam regime was a cancer on the Middle East, the president believed, and Saddam's ousting would help tremendously in bringing necessary reform and stability to the region.

Indeed, the president had become singularly focused on removing the Iraqi dictator by any means necessary. "He was not going to be easily deterred or distracted," one of the president's senior advisors told a reporter. "It would have taken nothing less than an Iraqi capitulation. Either Saddam and his inner circle would have had to leave or they would have had to really, truly, completely, verifiably disarm. Bottom line: Bush was not looking for a way out."

On December 7, Iraq presented the United Nations with a 12,000-page report on its weapons of mass destruction programs, as required by the Security Council resolution. White House officials were immediately skeptical and began poring over the document looking for lapses, lies and misinformation. Few believed the report truthfully revealed the full extent of Iraq's weapons of mass destruction.

Later the same day, Saddam let loose a flood of crocodile tears as he apologized to the people of Kuwait for invading their country more than a decade earlier. White House officials scoffed at the dictator's too-little/too-late effort to gain international acceptance as a man of remorse.

A month later, the Pentagon initiated the creation of a headquarters staff in the tiny country of Qatar — the first step toward invasion of Iraq. Shortly afterward, Secretary Rumsfeld signed an order authorizing the gradual deployment of 130,000 troops to the Gulf region. The message to Saddam was clear: We're coming to get you.

Later in January, Secretary Rumsfeld suggested another peaceful alternative to war — exile for Saddam. In his usual no-nonsense manner, Secretary Rumsfeld stated that war could be averted and the dictator's life spared if Saddam and his family packed up and moved to another country. As expected, Iraqi officials scoffed at the notion. Saddam wasn't going anywhere, they said. If the United States wanted him out, it would have to come and take him out. Which, of course, was the president's intention all along.

When the protracted weapons inspections ultimately proved futile, President Bush and British Prime Minister Tony Blair asked for a second U.N. resolution approving military action against Iraq. On February 5, in a lengthy address before the U.N. Security Council, Secretary Powell methodically listed Iraq's past transgressions in great detail and presented what he said was absolute proof that Saddam was a clear and present danger to his people and the entire world.

Secretary Powell approached the address with the dedicated resolve of a trial attorney trying to convict a heinous criminal. He desperately wanted to convince the skeptical members of the Security Council that Saddam had to be taken out — and quickly. Following are several enlightening excerpts from Secretary Powell's address regarding Iraq's weapons of mass destruction and its suspected association with terrorist groups:

"Our conservative estimate is that Iraq today has a stockpile of between 100 and 150 tons of chemical-weapons agent. That is enough agent to fill 16,000 battlefield rockets. Even the low end of 100 tons of agent would enable Saddam Hussein to cause mass casualties across more than 100 square miles of territory, an area nearly five times the size of Manhattan.

"Let me remind you (about) the 122-millimeter chemical warheads that the U.N. inspectors found (on January 16). This discovery could very well be, as has been noted, the tip of a submerged iceberg. The question before us all, my friends, is, when will we see the rest of the submerged iceberg?

"Saddam Hussein has chemical weapons. Saddam Hussein has used such weapons. And Saddam Hussein has no compunction about using them again — against his neighbors and against his own people. And we have sources who tell us that he recently has authorized his field commanders to use them. He wouldn't be passing out the orders if he didn't have the weapons or the intent to use them.

"We also have sources who tell us that since the 1980s, Saddam's regime has been experimenting on human beings to perfect its biological or chemical weapons. A source said that 1,600 death-row prisoners were transferred in 1995 to a special unit for such experiments. An eyewitness saw prisoners tied down to beds, experiments conducted on them, blood oozing around the victims' mouths and autopsies performed to confirm the effects on the prisoners. Saddam Hussein's inhumanity has no limits."

Secretary Powell then addressed the even more terrifying subject of Saddam Hussein's quest for nuclear weapons:

"We have no indication that Saddam Hussein has ever abandoned his nuclear-weapons program. On the contrary, we have more than a decade of proof that he remains determined to acquire nuclear weapons.

"To fully appreciate the challenge that we face today, remember that in 1991, the inspectors searched Iraq's primary nuclear weapons facility for the first time and they found nothing to conclude that Iraq had a nuclear-weapons program. But based on defector information, in May of 1991 Saddam Hussein's lie was exposed. In truth, Saddam Hussein had a massive clandestine nuclear weapons program that covered several different techniques to enrich uranium, including electromagnetic isotope separation, gas centrifuge and gas diffusion.

"We estimate that this illicit program cost the Iraqis several billion dollars. Nonetheless, Iraq continues to tell the IAEA that it had no nuclear weapons program. If Saddam had not been stopped, Iraq would have produced a nuclear bomb by 1993, years earlier than most worst-case assessments ...

"In 1995, as a result of another defector, we found out that after his invasion of Kuwait, Saddam Hussein had initiated a crash program to build a crude nuclear weapon in violation of Iraq's U.N. obligations. Saddam Hussein already possesses two out of the three key components needed to build a nuclear bomb. He has a cadre of nuclear scientists with the expertise and he has a bomb design. Since 1998, his efforts to reconstitute his nuclear program have been focused on acquiring the third and last component — sufficient fissile material to produce a nuclear explosion ...

"Saddam Hussein is determined to get his hands on a nuclear bomb. He is so determined that he has made repeated covert attempts to acquire high-specification aluminum tubes from 11 different countries, even after inspections resumed. These tubes are controlled by the Nuclear Suppliers Group precisely because they can be used as centrifuges for enriching uranium.

"... People will continue to debate this issue, but there is no doubt in my mind, these illicit procurement efforts show that Saddam Hussein is very much focused on putting in place the key missing piece from his nuclear weapons program, the ability to produce fissile material. He also has been busy trying to maintain the other key parts of his nuclear program, particularly his cadre of key nuclear scientists. It is noteworthy that over the last 18 months, Saddam Hussein has paid increasing personal attention to Iraq's top nuclear scientists, a group that the government-controlled press calls openly, his 'nuclear mujaheddin.' He regularly exhorts them and praises their progress. Progress toward what end? Long ago, the Security Council — this council — required Iraq to halt all nuclear activities of any kind."

Secretary Powell went on to offer proof that Saddam was actively pursuing the creation of chemical and biological weapons — again in direct defiance of the 1991 U.N. resolution:

"To support its deadly biological and chemical weapons programs, Iraq procures needed items from around the world, using an extensive clandestine network. What we know comes largely from intercepted communications and human sources who are in a position to know the facts.

"Iraq's procurement efforts include equipment that can filter and separate microorganisms and toxins involved in biological weapons; equipment that can be used to concentrate the agent; growth media that can be used to continue producing anthrax and botulinum toxin; sterilization equipment for laboratories; glass-lined reactors and specialty pumps that can handle corrosive chemical weapons agents and precursors; large amounts of thionyl chloride, a precursor for nerve and blister agents, and other chemicals, such as sodium sulfide, an important mustard agent precursor.

"Now of course Iraq will argue that these items can also be used for legitimate purposes. But if that is true, why did we have to learn about them by intercepting communications and risking the lives of human agents? With Iraq's well-documented history of biological and chemical weapons, why should any of us give Iraq the benefit of the doubt?"

Secretary Powell also discussed the methods by which Iraq could deliver its weapons of mass destruction:

"We all remember that before the Gulf War, Saddam Hussein's goal was missiles that flew not just hundreds, but thousands of kilometers. He wanted to strike not only his neighbors, but also nations far beyond his borders. While inspectors destroyed most of the prohibited ballistic missiles, numerous intelligence reports over the past decade from sources inside Iraq indicate that Saddam Hussein retains a covert force of up to a few dozen Scud-variant ballistic missiles. These are missiles with a range of 650 to 900 kilometers.

"We knew from intelligence and Iraq's own admissions that Iraq's alleged permitted ballistic missiles, the al-Samoud 2 and the al-Fatah, violate the 150-kilometer limit established by this council in Resolution 687. These are prohibited systems. The United Nations Monitoring, Verification and Inspection Commission (UNMOVIC) has also reported that Iraq has illegally imported 380 SA-2 rocket engines. These are likely for use in the al-Samoud 2.

"... What I want you to know today is that Iraq has programs that are intended to produce ballistic missiles that fly over 1,000 kilometers. One program is pursuing a liquid-fuel missile that would be able to fly more than 1,200 kilometers. And you can see from this map as well as I can who will be in danger of these missiles.

"...Saddam Hussein's intentions have never changed. He is not developing the missiles for self-defense. These are missiles that Iraq wants in order to project power, to threaten and to deliver chemical, biological and, if we let him, nuclear warheads.

"Now, (about) unmanned aerial vehicles, UAVs ... (These) are well suited for dispensing chemical and biological weapons. There is ample evidence that Iraq has dedicated much effort to developing and testing spray devices adapted for UAVs. And in the little that Saddam Hussein has told us about UAVs, he has not told the truth.

"... My friends, the information I have presented to you about these terrible weapons and about Iraq's continued flaunting of its obligations under Security Council Resolution 1441 links to a subject I now want to spend a little bit of time on and that has to do with terrorism. Our concern is not just about these illicit weapons; it's the way that these illicit weapons can be connected to terrorists and terrorist organizations that have no compunction about using such devices against innocent people around the world. Iraq and terrorism go back decades. Baghdad trains Palestine Liberation Front members in small arms and explosives. Saddam uses the Arab Liberation Front to funnel money to the families of Palestinian suicide bombers in order to prolong the intifada (Palestinian uprising). And it's no secret that Saddam's own intelligence service was involved in dozens of attacks or attempted assassinations in the 1990s.

"But what I want to bring to your attention today is the potentially much more sinister nexus between Iraq and the al Qaeda terrorist network, a nexus that combines classic terrorist organizations and modern methods of murder. Iraq today harbors a deadly terrorist network, headed by Abu Mussab al-Zarqawi, an associate and collaborator of Osama bin Laden and his al Qaeda lieutenants ... We are not surprised that Iraq is harboring Zarqawi and his subordinates. This understanding builds on decades-long experience with respect to ties between Iraq and al Qaeda."

Lastly, Secretary Powell addressed the issue of Iraq's appalling human rights record:

"Underlying all that I have said, underlying all of the facts and the patterns of behavior that I have identified is Saddam Hussein's contempt for the will of this council, his contempt for the truth and, most damning of all, his utter contempt for human life.

"Saddam Hussein's use of mustard gas and nerve gas against the Kurds in 1988 was one of the 20th century's most horrible atrocities. Five thousand men, women and children died. His campaign against the Kurds from 1987 to '89 included mass summary executions, disappearances, arbitrary jailing, ethnic cleansing and the destruction of some 2,000 villages. He has also conducted ethnic cleansing against the Shiite Iraqis and the Marsh Arabs, whose culture has flourished for more than a millennium.

"Saddam Hussein's police state ruthlessly eliminates anyone who dares to dissent. Iraq has more forced disappearance cases than any other country — tens of thousands of people reported missing in the past decade.

"Nothing points more clearly to Saddam Hussein's dangerous intentions and the threat he poses to all of us than his calculated cruelty to his own citizens and to his neighbors. Clearly, Saddam Hussein and his regime will stop at nothing until something stops him.

"For more than 20 years, by word and by deed, Saddam Hussein has pursued his ambitions to dominate Iraq and the broader Middle East using the only means he knows — intimidation, coercion and annihilation of all those who might stand in his way. For Saddam Hussein, possession of the world's most deadly weapons is the ultimate trump card, the one he must hold to fulfill his ambition.

"We know that Saddam Hussein is determined to keep his weapons of mass destruction. He's determined to make more. Given Saddam Hussein's history of aggression, given what we know of his grandiose plans, given what we know of his terrorist associations and given his determination to exact revenge on those who oppose him, should we take the risk that he will not someday use these weapons at a time and a place and in a manner of his choosing, at a time when the world is in a much weaker position to respond?

"The United States will not and cannot run that risk to the American people. Leaving Saddam Hussein in possession of weapons of mass destruction for a few more months or years is not an option, not in a post-September 11th world.

"... My colleagues, we have an obligation to our citizens, we have an obligation to this body to see that our resolutions are complied with. We wrote 1441 not in order to go to war; we wrote 1441 to try to preserve the peace. We wrote 1441 to give Iraq one last chance. Iraq is not, so far, taking this one last chance. We must not shrink from whatever is ahead of us. We must not fail in our duty and our responsibility for the citizens of the countries that are represented by this body."

Following Secretary Powell's damning indictment, Saddam continued his half-hearted attempt at appeasing the U.N. Security Council by making a great show out of the destruction of a handful of al-Samoud 2 missiles. However, the White House was unimpressed and continued to amass troops in the region for what seemed like an inevitable military showdown.

On February 26, the CBS newsmagazine *60 Minutes* aired an interview with Saddam conducted by Dan Rather. It was a coup for the network, though some critics accused Rather of lobbing softball questions at the dictator. During the interview, Rather asked Saddam if he expected to be attacked by an American-led invasion. Through an interpreter, Saddam replied, "We hope that the attack will not take place, but we are bracing ourselves to meet such an attack. The officials in America keep talking about attacking Iraq and it's normal that the people prepare themselves for such a possibility. At the same time, they are praying to Allah to stop the Americans from going through with it and to spare the Iraqis from the harm that those on the bandwagon of evil want to inflict on them."

Rather followed up by asking Saddam if he was afraid of being captured or killed. His answer dripping with false morality, the Butcher of Baghdad answered: "Whatever Allah decides. We are believers. We believe in what he decides. There is no value for any life without faith. When we were young, we decided to place ourselves to the service of our people. We did not ask the question whether we were going to live or die. It's morally unacceptable to ask such a question. Nothing is going to change the will of God. The believer still believes that what God decides is acceptable."

The days seemed to pass quickly as a showdown with Iraq grew increasingly certain. Saddam continued to defy the United Nations, and members of the U.N. Security Council seemed unable to reach a satisfactory compromise on the issue. During a press conference on March 7, President

Bush again hammered home the need to take immediate action against Iraq:

"If the Iraqi regime were disarming, we would know it because we would see it. Iraq's weapons would be presented to inspectors and the world would witness their destruction. Instead, with the world demanding disarmament and more than 200,000 troops positioned near his country, Saddam Hussein's response is to produce a few weapons for show, while he hides the rest and builds even more.

"Inspection teams do not need more time or more personnel. All they need is what they have never received — the full cooperation of the Iraqi regime. Token gestures are not acceptable. The only acceptable outcome is the one already defined by a unanimous vote of the Security Council: total disarmament.

"Great Britain, Spain and the United States have introduced a new resolution stating that Iraq has failed to meet the requirements of Resolution 1441. Saddam Hussein is not disarming. This is a fact. It cannot be denied.

"Saddam Hussein has a long history of reckless aggression and terrible crimes. He possesses weapons of terror. He provides funding and training and safe haven to terrorists — terrorists who would willingly use weapons of mass destruction against America and other peace-loving countries. Saddam Hussein and his weapons are a direct threat to this country, to our people and to all free people.

"If the world fails to confront the threat posed by the Iraqi regime, refusing to use force even as a last resort, free nations could assume immense and unacceptable risks. The attacks of September 11, 2001, show what the enemies of America did with four airplanes. We will not wait to see what terrorists or terrorist states could do with weapons of mass destruction.

"We are determined to confront threats wherever they arise. I will not leave the American people at the mercy of the Iraqi dictator and his weapons. In the event of conflict, America also accepts our responsibility to protect innocent lives in every way possible. We will bring food and medicine to the people of Iraq. We will help that nation to build a just government after decades of brutal dictatorship. The form and leadership of that government is for the Iraqi people to choose. Anything they choose will be better than the misery and torture and murder they have known under Saddam Hussein.

"Across the world and in every part of America people of good will are hoping and praying for peace. Our goal is peace for our nation, for our friends and allies, for the people of the Middle East. People of good will must also recognize that allowing a dangerous dictator to defy the world and harbor weapons of mass murder and terror is not peace at all, it is pretense. The cause of peace will be advanced only when the terrorists lose a wealthy patron and protector, and when the dictator is fully and finally disarmed."

There was no denying the president's resolve. One way or the other — and sooner rather than later — Saddam's bloody regime would be no more.

CHAPTER SIX

"SHOCK AND AWE"

The time had come to remove Saddam Hussein once and for all.

President Bush and his advisors never believed that the Iraqi strongman would completely disarm, as demanded by the United Nations, or quietly leave the country and go into exile. That simply wasn't Saddam's way. He didn't become the iron-fisted ruler of Iraq by showing weakness to any enemy and he certainly wasn't going to start now. The only way to oust him was through military force.

In early March, while the United Nations worked desperately for a peaceful solution to the Iraq crisis, the U.S.-led coalition began amassing troops and equipment in the Persian Gulf region. Kuwait, which understandably held a seething hatred for Saddam, was more than willing to allow a buildup of troops on its bases, allowing for an easy invasion from the south. However, Turkey — vital for entering Iraq from the north — proved far less cooperative. Early in the game, it demanded billions of dollars in U.S. aid in exchange for use of its bases, a requirement many American officials felt was a form of diplomatic extortion.

By the middle of the month, with nearly 250,000 soldiers in the region and more on the way, coalition senior commanders outlined what they called a "rolling start" to the war, in which the invasion would begin even as additional troops and equipment continued to arrive. "We recognized from the very beginning that we were going to be fighting and building up combat power at about the same time," said Lt. Gen. William S. Wallace, the V Corps commander who would lead the Army's attack.

This blueprint was decidedly different from that of the first Gulf War. During that conflict, U.S. military leaders took six months to complete a massive military buildup, then weakened Iraqi occupation forces in Kuwait with a 39-day bombardment before going in. The strategy of overwhelming force quickly drove the Iraqi invaders back across the border.

Despite concerns from some former U.S. commanders that a greater force was necessary for a successful invasion of Iraq, coalition military leaders said they expected spectacular results using fewer men and more firepower — including many state-of-the-art weapons that had not been available in 1991. "When I look at the enemy, when I look at the terrain over which he's arrayed, I think we have adequate forces to do the job," Lt. Gen. Wallace said. "There seems to me to be a more (cohesive) joint fight this time with the air, naval and certainly a very pronounced Marine presence."

On March 16, President Bush, British Prime Minister Tony Blair and Spanish Prime Minister Jose Maria Aznar issued an ultimatum to the United Nations: They were ready to begin military action against Saddam with or without the endorsement of the international body.

The following day, in a televised address to the world, President Bush made a final attempt to oust Saddam without bloodshed. Leave Iraq within 48 hours, the president warned the Iraqi madman, or face the devastating power of the U.S. military. "This is not a question of authority," the president added, his face firm with resolve. "It's a matter of will."

Turning his attention to the people of Iraq, President Bush said: "The tyrant will soon be gone. The day of your liberation is near." He then warned the Iraqi military not to destroy oil wells or obey commands to use weapons of mass destruction. Those who did so, the president stated, would be hunted down and tried as war criminals.

President Bush's advisors were quick to acknowledge that there was virtually no chance Saddam and his family would voluntarily go into exile. In fact, Iraq summarily rejected the notion, with Iraqi Foreign Minister Naji Sabri commenting that the one who should leave was "the warmonger number one in the world, the failing President Bush, who made his country a joke." Saddam had faced hard foes before and, in his delusional state, no doubt believed he could actually win a war against the United States and its allies. Or, failing that, die a martyr — at least in his own eyes.

The president's speech had a second important purpose — it placed the entire world on notice that war in Iraq was just hours away. The message was clear: If you were in Iraq and wanted to go home, you had better pack your bags and get to the airport pronto because the bombs were soon going to fall. As a result, hundreds of diplomats, journalists and foreign workers fled the country. U.N. weapons inspectors and aid workers also prepared to leave.

In the United States, the president's declaration caused the Department of Homeland Security to raise the terrorism alert level to orange, indicating a high risk of attack. Security measures were strengthened nationwide in anticipation of retaliatory attacks by Iraqi agents or al Qaeda sleeper cells in the wake of military action against Iraq. Patrols at seaports, airports and nuclear power plants were increased and greater safeguards were placed on the nation's food supply. Americans, advised to hope for the best but plan for the worst, rushed to create home emergency kits.

For a day, the world waited. The hundreds of thousands of American and British troops amassed at the Iraqi border bided their time, waiting for orders from the president. Many took care of last-minute personal business, including letters to home. Meanwhile officials in Baghdad continued to ridicule the United States for even thinking that Saddam would flee. President Bush is the one who "should go into exile," crowed Naji Sabri, "because it is Mr. Bush who is endangering the whole world."

On the night of Wednesday, March 19, the United States landed the first punch of the war. However, it wasn't the massive bombardment of Baghdad that the entire world had anticipated. Instead, it was an extraordinarily precise attack using cruise missiles and guided bombs. Coalition commanders hoped the surgical strike would "decapitate" the Iraqi high command — specifically Saddam, his two equally crazy sons and other top Iraqi leaders — and bring the war to a quick and decisive end with a minimum of force.

In a televised address from the Oval Office, President Bush announced that the attack signaled "the early stages of military operations to disarm Iraq, to free its people and to defend the world from grave danger."

"Now that conflict has come," the president added, "the only way to limit its duration is to apply decisive force. And I assure you, this will not be a campaign of half measures and we will accept no outcome but victory."

The attempt on Saddam's life during the very first minutes of the war seemed like a scene from a Tom Clancy novel — and yet it was true. For months, the CIA and U.S. Special Forces had been trying to turn someone in Saddam's inner circle so they would have inside knowledge of Saddam's plans and — most importantly — his location. The latter information was tricky because Saddam seldom spent more than one or two nights at a particular location, preferring to stay on the move to confuse his enemies.

After much effort, the secret U.S. commando group known as Delta Force was able to recruit a senior Iraqi official who was close to Saddam and had accurate knowledge of his whereabouts. The Iraqi official had decided to aid the good guys because he knew a regime change was imminent and he feared the American war machine more than he feared Saddam — a man known to exact horrific revenge against anyone he even suspected of being disloyal.

The Iraqi turncoat told his American connections that on the night of March 19 Saddam and his sons would be sleeping in a bunker beneath a presidential compound in a quiet Baghdad neighborhood — one of several secure locations throughout Iraq's capital.

CIA Director George Tenet received the information around 3 p.m. EST (11 p.m. Iraq time) and raced to the Pentagon to brief Secretary of Defense Donald Rumsfeld, who was in the process of finalizing the air war that was scheduled to commence the following night. If the intelligence information was accurate and the United States acted quickly, it could end the war before it even started, potentially saving thousands of coalition and Iraqi lives.

Tenet, Secretary Rumsfeld and Gen. Richard Myers, chairman of the Joint Chiefs of Staff, crossed the Potomac River to the White House so they could brief President Bush. A few hours still remained before the deadline set for Saddam to flee the country, but the president dismissed that fact because he knew Saddam had no intention of leaving. Better to take out Saddam while they had the opportunity.

However, it wouldn't be easy. Saddam and his sons were believed to be sleeping in a bunker deep beneath the home — well protected from conventional missiles. So-called "bunker-busters" — 2,000-pound MK-84s — would be necessary to get the job done.

On the president's OK, Gen. Tommy Franks ordered into the air two F-117 stealth fighters, each carrying two bunker-buster bombs. They were instructed to fly toward Iraq but not enter Iraqi airspace until ordered to do so. Meanwhile, 40 cruise missiles on eight American ships in the Persian Gulf were fed the precise coordinates of Saddam's suspected location. Though not as powerful as the bunker-busters, they could still inflict a lot of damage and hopefully eliminate any survivors.

Just three minutes before the deadline imposed by Gen. Franks, President Bush ordered the plan into action. The stealth bombers easily eluded Iraqi air defenses and dropped their bombs around 5:30 a.m. local time. A CIA spy situated near the presidential home confirmed that Saddam was inside at the time of the attack and that rescue workers were desperately digging through the rubble. Word was that Saddam had, at the very least, been wounded in the attack, but no one could confirm that information.

The following morning, on Thursday, March 20, confusion mounted when a man purported to be Saddam appeared on Iraqi television to condemn the airstrike and call for his people to "draw your swords" against the coming invaders. The individual, wearing a beret and thick glasses, looked haggard as he read from a notebook and some analysts suspected he was one of the many doubles trained to impersonate Saddam over the years.

Despite Saddam's call to arms, it was obvious that the majority of Iraqis didn't want to fight and in fact couldn't wait for coalition forces to liberate them from their leader's bloody clutches. In the days prior to the beginning of the war, there were numerous reports of Iraqi soldiers begging to surrender to coalition forces just across the border in Kuwait, only to be told to go home because the war hadn't officially started.

The preliminary air war gave way to a land invasion throughout that Thursday as American and British forces poured into Iraq from Kuwait. Some resistance was encountered. The 1st Marine Division reported destroying an Iraqi T-55 tank with an antitank missile and the U.S. Army 3rd Infantry Division launched self-propelled howitzers and other weapons against various Iraqi targets.

That evening, more cruise missiles were lobbed

into Baghdad in an attempt to destroy key government and military installations, disable communications systems and apply additional pressure against Saddam and key government leaders. One bombardment left the Ministry of Planning in flames. For much of the night, bombs, tracers and antiaircraft fire lit up the night sky like a Fourth of July fireworks display, proving beyond doubt that Saddam was a doomed man and that his reign of terror would soon be over.

In response to the bombardment, Iraqi forces fired several missiles at U.S. and British forces in the desert and toward Kuwait City. At least two missiles were shot down by a Patriot antimissile system and there were no reports of damage or casualties. Fearful that the missiles might contain chemical or biological agents, American troops and Kuwaiti citizens donned protective suits and gas masks every time air raid sirens sounded.

Now that it was in full swing, everyone hoped the conflict would be over quickly. However, the White House emphasized that the true nature of the war remained to be seen and that "it will take as long as it takes." Caution was the watchword, military officials emphasized, and nothing regarding the war was carved in granite.

In a report to Congress, President Bush justified the invasion as necessary and legal under international law. Deposing Saddam, he explained, would help disable Middle East terrorism and bring stability to the region. "The United States has clear authority to use military force against Iraq to assure its national security and to compel Iraq's compliance with applicable U.N. Security Council resolutions," the report stated.

The Bush administration also called for a worldwide expulsion of Iraqi diplomats. According to State Department spokesman Richard Boucher, the diplomats represented "a corrupt and ruthless regime." Australia was one of the first nations to comply, giving Iraqi diplomats and their families just a few days to leave the country.

Once in Iraq, coalition forces worked furiously to gain ground and cripple the opposition. Waves of airstrikes were launched against strategic locations in several cities on Friday, March 21, signaling the beginning of the so-called "shock and awe" campaign designed to liberate the country with an overwhelming show of military strength.

The attacks began around 9 p.m. local time as hundreds of coalition aircraft dropped missiles and bombs on Saddam's presidential palaces, ministerial buildings and military targets in Baghdad, Kirkuk, Mosul and Tikrit. In addition, warships and submarines in the Persian Gulf and the Red Sea bombarded targets with more than 300 Tomahawk missiles.

Secretary of Defense Rumsfeld told reporters that the massive bombardment was ordered only after senior Iraqi officers refused to surrender. "It was the absolute last choice after every single other thing that could be done had been done," Secretary Rumsfeld explained, adding that the location and precision of the attacks was meant to minimize civilian casualties

Facing overwhelming opposition, huge numbers of Iraqi soldiers gave up without firing a shot during the first days of the war. In southern Iraq, hundreds of men with Iraq's 51st Infantry Division, assigned to defend Basra, gave up or simply left the battlefield. Most weren't members of Saddam's fabled Republican Guard, but a ragtag group, many conscripted against their will, who didn't want to die in defense of an unjust regime. After laying down their arms, many of those who surrendered were given food, water and medical care by American medics.

"I kind of felt sorry for them," said one U.S. military official. "A lot of them looked hungry. They haven't been fed for a while."

Less than 24 hours after rolling across the border, members of the Army's 3rd Infantry Division were a third of the way to Baghdad.

One of the prime objectives during the early days

of the war was the security of Iraq's vast oil fields. During the first Gulf War, Saddam's forces created an environmental nightmare when they ignited hundreds of Kuwaiti oil wells as they retreated back to Iraq and coalition forces wanted to make sure that didn't happen this time. President Bush and Secretary Rumsfeld issued stern warnings to Iraqi soldiers and only a couple of Iraqi oil wells appeared to have been intentionally set ablaze as coalition forces crossed the border.

Indeed, most of the news regarding Iraq's oil fields was good. On Friday, March 21, Navy SEALs, assisted by a small detachment of Polish special operations forces, successfully seized two Iraqi offshore oil terminals. Under the cloak of darkness, the highly trained commandos used quiet, high-speed jet boats to get from their base in Kuwait to the oil terminals, which were located about 25 miles off the Iraqi coast. Once aboard the platforms, the heavily armed force surprised Iraqi guards as they were apparently getting ready to go to bed. The guards put up no resistance and were quickly taken prisoner.

American officials wanted to take the terminals as quickly as possible because they were afraid that Saddam might torch them or open their spigots, dumping millions of barrels of oil into the Persian Gulf, just as he did in 1991. The leader of one of the SEAL teams said parts of the Mina al

Bakr terminal had been wired with explosives, but that the effort appeared "half-hearted" and the guards had apparently disobeyed orders to blow up the platform.

U.S. and British forces also captured several key facilities in Iraq's southern oil fields, protecting them for use during the beleaguered nation's postwar reconstruction. One of the most important was the Rumeila field west of Basra. With an output of 1.3 million barrels of oil a day, it was one of Iraq's most productive. The troops were also relieved to find that only seven of the field's hundreds of wells were on fire. Based on satellite images of the smoke covering the region, the number had been thought to be much higher.

"All the key components of the southern oil fields are safe now," announced Adm. Michael Boyce, chief of the British defense staff. "We have special civilian contractors on their way who will be in the area very shortly to deal with the oil well fires."

The ground assault continued at a brisk pace and by Saturday, March 22, coalition forces had crossed the Euphrates River and were nearly halfway to Baghdad, which continued to be pounded by airstrikes. Oil-filled trenches around the city were ignited in an effort to hide the city from air raids with smoke. However, the effort proved futile as high-tech missiles, guided by lasers and satellites able to pierce both darkness and smoke, continued to rain down. In southern Iraq, firefights were frequent as British and American troops headed north through the desert toward Baghdad. Many captured Iraqis were set free because their presence only slowed the race toward Iraq's capital city.

Of particular importance was the capture of a major highway bridge across the Euphrates River at Nasiriyah, taken after the seizure of the Tallil air base. Members of the Iraqi 11th Mechanized Infantry surrendered after putting up initial resistance. However, the next day remaining forces from that division engaged U.S. Marines on the outskirts of Nasiriyah in a day-long firefight that turned into some of the most vicious fighting of the war up to that time. The Marines fought with all they had, trying desperately to locate hidden Iraqi artillery. It was a deadly game of cat and mouse that proved Iraqi forces loyal to Saddam were far from beaten. In the end, the bridge — vital to the invasion of Baghdad — remained under American control, but strong resistance within the city itself confounded coalition forces for many days.

Meanwhile in the south near Basra, Iraq's second largest city, the Iraqi 51st Infantry Division surrendered to better-equipped coalition forces, leaving the city of 1.3 million guarded by a small but tenacious group of Saddam's security forces. For the time being, American and British forces decided not to occupy the city: "Military commanders do not engage in urban areas if they don't have to," explained British Col. Chris Vernon. "The objective is the capitulation of the Iraqi government."

In various battles, coalition forces found themselves facing cowardly guerrilla tactics, a clear indication of the Iraqi military's growing desperation. In one incident, Iraqis waving white flags of surrender opened fire on coalition forces as they drew near. In another, Iraqi soldiers in civilian clothes pretended to welcome American soldiers then suddenly attacked them. And in Nasiriyah, U.S. Marines reported that Iraqi soldiers were using women and children as human shields, as well as leaping out of supposedly civilian cars and taxis to shoot at them.

As coalition forces drew ever closer to Baghdad, Saddam tried to rally the faithful. In another of his crazed, delusional television speeches, he claimed "victory will soon be ours." During that address, Saddam — decked out in a military uniform — appealed to his people's nationalism by telling them that the United States had come not to liberate Iraq but to conquer it. "In these decisive days ... you Iraqis are in line with what God has ordered you to do, to cut their throats," he said. U.S. officials were unable to determine when the televised address had been taped.

At the Pentagon, Maj. Gen. Stanley McChrystal, vice director of operations for the Joint Chiefs of Staff, told reporters that the fighting was expected to grow increasingly intense as coalition forces arrived at the outskirts of Baghdad. Still waiting was the Republican Guard's Medina Division, one of Iraq's best units and what McChrystal described as the "linchpin" in Saddam's defense of the city. It was hoped that frequent air attacks would soften the Republican Guard and make their defeat a little easier for coalition forces.

No one expected Baghdad to fall easily. Though most Baghdadis awaited their liberation with great anticipation, those defending the city were fanatical supporters of Saddam — many of them members of the Fedayeen Saddam paramilitary group — and they were expected to put up a tremendous fight.

The general plan called for American-led forces to lay siege to Baghdad and completely isolate it from the rest of the country. Once an impenetrable perimeter was established, the military noose would tighten until Saddam was captured or killed. However, Secretary of Defense Rumsfeld said officials were hopeful that the people of Iraq would rise up against Saddam before U.S. troops had to invade the city.

With the war at full force and progressing steadily, the number of Iraqi civilians left without food, water or shelter grew by the day. However, Iraqi resistance prevented relief organizations from delivering the desperately needed supplies. Ships and warehouses around the Persian Gulf were piled to the ceiling with food rations, clean water, medical supplies and temporary shelters, but they couldn't be delivered until U.S. and British minesweepers cleared a path for the supply ships in the deep-water port of Umm Qasr and connecting waterways, and the land passage to those in need was deemed safe.

It wasn't as easy as it seemed. A week after the start of the war, skirmishes around Umm Qasr, Basra and other regions continued to keep supply shipments at bay. In many areas, clean drinking water had become extremely scarce and humanitarian officials feared outbreaks of cholera and other deadly diseases if the situation wasn't addressed quickly. Their concerns were well-founded — during the first Gulf War, a lengthy lack of electricity and clean water resulted in outbreaks of devastating pestilence that killed hundreds.

Even in their final days, it seemed, Saddam and his supporters were able to inflict one last indignity on the people of Iraq.

On Tuesday, March 25, U.S. ground troops moved to within striking distance of Republican

Guard divisions defending Baghdad — despite a severe sandstorm that limited visibility and damaged equipment.

In a day-long assault designed to soften enemy resistance, the Army's 3rd Infantry Division bombarded targets just 50 miles south of Baghdad with howitzers and rockets. B-52 bombers also did their part to weaken the Medina Division of the elite Republican Guard as coalition troops drew ever nearer to their goal.

Meanwhile, British forces moved against civilian militia and paramilitary Fedayeen Saddam units in Basra. The soldiers had spent days engaged in running tank and artillery battles with die-hard Iraqi forces on the outskirts of the city, but did not enter it because of the tremendous risk to civilians. When British military officials finally declared armed elements within the city a military target, they went in. British commanders reported finding groups of terrified civilians being used as shields by the Fedayeen Saddam forces.

In other areas, Iraqi artillery was used against civilians protesting against Saddam. "Iraqi civilians are being killed on the battlefield by Iraqis," confirmed U.S. Army Brig. Gen. Vincent Brooks. "The regime has shown its true colors the last few days of fighting."

In the days that followed, U.S. forces quickly advanced on Baghdad, encountering stiff resistance from Saddam loyalists along the way. The battle for Baghdad — and the end of Saddam's regime — was taking shape.

During the advance, Iraqi prisoners of war detailed for their American captors the extreme desperation of Saddam's military leaders. Many of the captured soldiers said they literally fought with guns to their heads because Saddam loyalists threatened to kill anyone who did not take up arms against the coalition forces. It wasn't an idle threat — dead Iraqis that had been found with bullet holes in the backs of their heads proved the extent of the Saddam regime's barbarism.

"The officers threatened to shoot us unless we fought," one wounded Iraqi sobbed to reporters in a field hospital. "They took out their guns and pointed them and told us to fight." Another Iraqi soldier said his superiors threatened to go after his family if he refused to join the war.

Ten days into the war, fierce fighting between U.S. forces and Iraqi soldiers and paramilitary continued in many cities. Basra was particularly hard hit, with hundreds of residents fleeing the city.

Baghdad continued to be the target of massive bombardment by cruise missiles and at least two 2,000-pound bunker- buster bombs. Damaged in the attacks were the Iraqi Information Ministry and an office of Saddam's brutal Baath Party.

While the bombs blasted away at the infrastructure of Saddam's ruthless regime, a quieter weapon was at work within the nation's capital. Covert teams from the CIA's paramilitary division, often assisted by the Iraqi underground, used stealth and daring to secretly assassinate members of Saddam's inner circle, including Baath Party officials and commanders of the Republican Guard.

According to U.S. officials, the teams included demolition experts as well as highly skilled snipers able to take down a target from hundreds of yards away. CIA units and special operations teams — part of the "invisible war" not shown on television — also helped organize tribal groups to fight the Iraqi government in the north as well as hunt down weapons of mass destruction.

Fifteen days into the war came news of the heroic rescue of Pfc. Jessica Lynch, a 19-year-old supply clerk with the 507th Maintenance Company who had been taken prisoner by the Iraqis after her convoy made a wrong turn in Nasiriyah on March 23. According to military officials, Lynch, a native of Palestine, W. Va., fought the enemy with extraordinary valor, firing her weapon until she ran out of ammunition. Unfortunately, others in Lynch's company died in the ambush.

The rescue took place after an Iraqi pharmacist walked several miles to tell U.S. military personnel that Lynch was being held at Saddam Hussein Hospital. The Iraqi gave soldiers a map of the hospital, noting the room in which Lynch was being kept, as well as information on the number and location of Iraqi soldiers.

Using information from CIA operatives, a Special Operations force of Navy SEALS, Army Rangers and Air Force combat controllers touched down at the medical facility in blackout conditions around midnight on April 1. An AC-130 gunship circled overhead, along with a reconnaissance plane that provided real-time video imagery of the daring rescue.

"There was shooting going in; there was shooting going out," said one military officer who had been briefed on the event. "It was not intensive. There was no shooting in the building, but it was hairy because no one knew what to expect. When they got inside, I don't think there was any resistance. (The building) was fairly abandoned."

Lynch, who had been injured during her capture, was placed on a stretcher and rushed to the waiting Black Hawk helicopter, which flew her and the rescue team to safety. Lynch was then flown to a military hospital in Germany. In her hometown, news of Lynch's rescue — the first successful rescue of an American POW since

World War II — was greeted with cheers of joy. Many of her friends and family had decorated neighborhood trees with yellow ribbons following news of her disappearance.

Jessica Lynch was one of the lucky ones. Throughout the early days of the war, there were numerous reports of abuses against American and British prisoners of war by Iraqi forces. In direct violation of the Geneva Convention, Iraqi military officials paraded POWs through towns, broadcast pictures of them over Iraqi television and subjected them to physical and mental abuse. Evidence also indicated that prisoners of war were being kept in filthy quarters and were not given adequate food, water or medical attention.

Worst of all, there was very strong evidence that American POWs had been summarily executed by their captors — yet another example of the complete disregard for human life that had come to characterize the Saddam regime. Television images of dead American soldiers strongly suggested they did not die in combat, but had been murdered after their capture.

The remarkable rescue of Jessica Lynch seemed to make coalition forces even more determined to roll into Baghdad and hunt down Saddam. On Wednesday, April 2, thousands of U.S. Army troops and Marines faced Republican Guard divisions on the southern roads to the capital. Three brigades of the Army's 3rd Infantry Division raced toward a Republican Guard division southwest of Baghdad while hundreds of Marines took on a Republican Guard division to the southeast.

Said Lt. Col. George Smith at Marine combat headquarters in Iraq: "We continue to tighten the noose around Baghdad."

The goal of the attack was to aggressively strip Saddam's remaining defenses around Baghdad and clear the way for a coalition invasion. It was hoped that Saddam's own men would turn on him in the face of overwhelming American and British forces, thus eliminating the need for door-to-door fighting. However, military officials said they had no idea what to expect once they entered Baghdad: They could be greeted with cheers and accolades or they might face dangerous pockets of resistance that could make the invasion — and Saddam's ultimate capture — extremely difficult.

Despite the very best in intelligence and technology, Saddam's whereabouts remained a perplexing puzzle. Was he wounded or in good health? What control did he still have over his troops and inner circle? If cornered, would he flee, fight to the death or take the coward's way out like Adolf Hitler did and take his own miserable life?

There was also the very serious question of chemical and biological weapons. Saddam had sworn he possessed no weapons of mass destruction, but materials and secret laboratories discovered throughout Iraq by coalition forces strongly suggested he had been lying. As a result, the specter of chemical death hung over every military action — particularly as forces approached Baghdad. The biggest fear among coalition military leaders was that Saddam would order the use of weapons of mass destruction as one final, vengeful act against the world.

It was clear that Saddam's regime was starting to feel the heat from the approaching American and British forces. Iraqi officials issued what they claimed was a personal plea by Saddam that Iraqis fight to the death in defense of their leader and their country. Oddly, Saddam did not appear in person to read the message. Instead, the statement was read by Information Minister al-Sahhaf.

"Those who are martyred will be rewarded in heaven," the statement said. "Seize the opportunity, my brothers."

As massive bombings and ground attacks methodically chiseled away at the Republican Guard forces protecting Baghdad, American and British military leaders prepared for the final confrontation — an all-out siege of the ancient city designed to wipe out any resistance with lightning-quick commando raids and missile attacks by helicopters and unmanned drones. "It's an age-old military tactic," said a senior Pentagon official. "This will be the endgame."

Saddam had learned an important lesson during the first Gulf War, in which he lost a tremendous number of men and equipment in a desert war that had strongly favored the technologically superior American forces. Anticipating another war with the United States, Saddam and his military advisors had practically ignored the desert in favor of defending the capital, knowing full well that an urban combat scenario placed coalition forces at a deadly disadvantage.

Though American troops were well-trained in house-to-house fighting, military leaders were extremely reluctant to engage the enemy that way. Urban combat always favored the sneaky guerrilla fighter, especially when the fighting was on his turf. Tanks and helicopters were limited in their movement and were easy targets for enemy soldiers carrying shoulder-launched mortars. The risk of civilian casualties was also much higher in urban combat and Saddam's supporters had already proved themselves more than willing to place innocents in harm's way.

As coalition forces began the difficult job of isolating Baghdad, British Prime Minister Tony Blair made the world aware of yet another cowardly tactic by Saddam and his henchmen —

damaging Muslim holy sites in Iraq and blaming the destruction on British and American forces. Even as Prime Minister Blair announced, "I would like to emphasize to the House of Commons and the wider Arab and Muslim world — we are doing everything we can to protect those holy sites and shrines," in a bizarre moment of synchronicity, Iraqi Information Minister al-Sahhaf was proclaiming that U.S. and British forces were trying to destroy mosques in Karbala and Najaf.

Al-Sahhaf's claim was a complete lie. U.S. commanders said that Iraqi soldiers in Najaf had repeatedly fired on U.S. forces from inside the Ali mosque, one of the world's most important Shiite shrines. But in deference to the mosque's religious significance, U.S. troops had not returned fire.

U.S. troops entered the outskirts of Baghdad on Thursday, April 3, bringing the ground war closer to Saddam than ever before. The Army's 3rd Infantry tank battalions headed a two-pronged assault, approaching the city from the southwest while the 1st Marine Division pushed toward Baghdad's outlying suburbs in the southeast.

As American ground forces took possession of Saddam International Airport and continued to soften resistance with regular artillery fire, Iraqi government officials scoffed at their approach. "They are not any place," laughed Minister of Information al-Sahhaf. "They are a snake moving in the desert. They hold no place in Iraq. This is an illusion."

In a desperate attempt to prove that he was still in control, Saddam — or a very good look-alike — was shown on Iraqi television Friday evening walking through a Baghdad neighborhood greeting passers-by and kissing babies as if he were a campaigning politician on a morning stroll. The dictator appeared relaxed and even cheerful during the 12-minute video that, again, gave no indication of when it had been taped. It was great propaganda from a man whose picture was featured on almost every public building in the nation, but few Iraqis saw it because many portions of the city no longer had electricity.

The next morning, on Saturday, April 5, more than 40 U.S. tanks and armored vehicles entered Baghdad for the very first time, parading through the southwestern section of the capital in a display of military might designed to show the nation that despite government reports, the city was no longer under Saddam's complete control. The raid drew strong resistance from Iraqi fighters, though no coalition forces were injured in the attacks. Following the raid — which Iraqi officials denied had occurred — the Iraqis quickly deployed tanks and field artillery to Baghdad and aimed at the southern, northern and western entrances, which they believed American forces would use to take the city.

In another demonstration that Baghdad was slowly but surely coming under coalition control, Saddam International Airport, located about 10 miles from the city, was renamed Baghdad International Airport and transformed into an American base as troops ringed the city and guarded major highways to ensure that Saddam and members of his inner circle did not try to slip away.

Also that day, British forces reported a gruesome discovery near Zubayr — a warehouse packed with hundreds of boxes containing human remains. The British press initially reported that the dead men and women had been victims of Saddam's regime — brutally tortured then summarily executed. However, a further investigation concluded that they were more likely the uninterred remains of Iraqi soldiers killed in the 1980s during the war with Iran. In total, the warehouse contained 664 caskets and 408 sets of human remains. There was no explanation for why they had not been buried.

As American forces systematically tightened the noose around Baghdad, strategists in Washington expressed fear that Saddam might

disappear into the complex warren of tunnels and
bunkers that lay deep beneath the streets of the
city. Built over a period of 20 years, the structures
were designed to protect Saddam, his family and
key government leaders against ground and air
attacks. It's believed that most of Saddam's
palaces had fortified bunkers beneath them, all
protected by blast doors and incredibly thick
walls of steel and concrete.

It was reported that many of the bunkers were
designed and built by a Serbian engineering firm
once run by the Yugoslav military. Saddam had
maintained close ties with Communist leader
Josip Tito and later with military strongman
Slobodan Milosevic who, like Saddam, ruled
his nation through torture and intimidation.
Milosevic also constructed a series of tunnels
and bunkers beneath his homes and they proved
particularly vexing to U.S. and NATO forces sent
to bring down the dictator during the 1999 war in
Kosovo.

The greatest fear was that Saddam and some of
his elite forces would try to hide in the underground maze, forcing American forces to hunt
them down tunnel by tunnel, room by room. Such
a mission would be perilous, so coalition forces did
their best to reduce the chance of Saddam going
underground by dropping powerful bunker-
buster bombs on known presidential sites.

With each passing day, American and British forces captured more and more Iraqi territory, though resistance in many areas was extremely tough.

After five days of heavy fighting, the U.S. Army took control of Karbala on Sunday, April 6, finally routing hundreds of entrenched Fedayeen Saddam fighters with continuous airstrikes and artillery fire. The victory drew cheers from the city's Shiite residents, and a crowd of 10,000 Saddam-haters quickly gathered in the public square to celebrate their liberation by pulling down a 20-foot bronze statue of the despised dictator. "Saddam is no more!" the throng chanted as the statue came crashing down. "Saddam is dead!"

The statue had been erected shortly after Saddam took power and tearful residents took turns stomping joyously on its face as it lay in the dirt. "We have been living in fear for so many years and we have been taught in the schools that Saddam would never die," said 20-year-old Hassan Muhammed, one of the many who pulled on the rope that brought the statue down. "This is a historic day and we will celebrate this day always."

In Basra, British forces took control of the city's power plant, municipal airport and key intersections, overwhelming enemy resistance with an

impressive column of 40 tanks and armored
personnel carriers.

To the north, an estimated 1,000 Kurdish militiamen, aided by coalition forces, stormed the
town of Ain Sifne in a push toward the city of
Mosul and the region's huge oilfields. After days
of fighting, the Kurds had advanced to within 20
miles of Mosul and were equally close to Kirkuk,
the site of another major oil field.

Meanwhile, the battle for Baghdad progressed
with remarkable speed. Iraqis fled by the thousands as American forces moved to isolate the city
and seek out and destroy enemy resistance.
Forays into the capital became increasingly bold,
though Iraqi officials maintained that the
Americans had been repulsed. "We beat them
back out of the airport," Iraqi Information
Secretary al-Sahhaf said. "We continued bom-
barding them with missiles and heavy artillery."

Of course, such was not the case. Television
images showed American forces in full control
of the airport and moving rapidly westward to
consolidate their positions.

In Salman Pak, a town approximately 20 miles
southeast of Baghdad, Marines of the 3rd
Battalion, 7th Marines, stormed the headquarters
of the Republican Guard's Second Corps, seized
another of Saddam's palaces and destroyed what
appeared to be a terrorist training camp, com-

plete with mock buildings and the interior of an airplane.

On Monday, April 7, in a repeat of the first strike of the war, American bombers dropped four precision-guided bunker-busters on a home in the quiet Mansour neighborhood of Baghdad because intelligence indicated that Saddam was meeting his two sons and other government leaders there. The bombs annihilated the targeted home and other nearby buildings and blasted a crater 60 feet wide and 30 feet deep.

"We can confirm that a leadership target has been struck," said U.S. military spokesman Lt. Cmdr. Charles Owens at U.S. Central Command in Qatar. "We have absolutely no way to confirm that Saddam Hussein was inside."

The swiftness of the assault was astounding — the bombs struck their targets just 45 minutes after intelligence sources informed U.S. military officers that Saddam was believed to be inside the building.

The attack was just another indicator that, one way or the other, Saddam was a doomed man. U.S. Army soldiers drove home the point by spending the night in one of the dictator's primary presidential palaces while 10,000 Marines fanned out through the outskirts of Baghdad. "The hostilities phase is coming to a conclusion," said Secretary of State Powell as the Iraqi military and government fell into further disarray.

The capture and occupation of the New Presidential Palace in Baghdad was a clear sign to the Iraqis that American forces were not only in their city but that they were there to stay. Located near Saddam's Baath Party headquarters, the palace had the opulence of a five-star hotel, said the soldiers who took up camp there. The troops immediately began searching the palace for intelligence material, and turned the palace compound into a processing center for Iraqi prisoners of war.

But it wasn't all serious business for the soldiers. They made good use of Saddam's gilded bathrooms — for some, the first indoor plumbing they had seen in many months. Exhausted from their swift drive through the desert, the soldiers marveled at the opulence of the residences and even took the chance to relax upon the lavish furniture. As the Iraqi people starved, Saddam had treated himself well, although now it was Americans enjoying the palaces that, for the most part, lay in ruins. "This used to be a nice place," joked Spc. Robert Blake, a member of the 3rd Battalion, 7th Infantry Regiment. "They should make it like a Six Flags or something."

The good news continued with an announcement by U.S. and British officials that Ali Hassan al-Majid — "Chemical Ali" — had almost certainly been killed in an allied bombing raid in Basra. "We believe that the reign of terror of Chemical Ali has come to an end," said Secretary of Defense Rumsfeld. "To Iraqis who have suffered at his hand, he will never again terrorize you or your families."

In Albu Muhawish, a small village located between Karbala and Hillah, American soldiers discovered barrels of what appeared to be deadly chemical agents — the kind that Saddam had long sworn he did not possess. Initial field tests and, later, secondary tests both confirmed the presence of the nerve agents Sarin and Tabun and the dangerous blister agent Lewsite at an agricultural warehouse located about two miles from a military compound. The chemicals, which were found in a recently constructed, partially buried bunker, were later flown to the United States to determine if they were weapons grade.

The discovery followed a search of the surrounding areas after soldiers stationed at the military base reported dizziness and vomiting. The stricken soldiers, who were guarding the facility, were decontaminated with full-body scrubdowns with bleach detergent and brushes after field tests detected Sarin.

The barrels were potentially the strongest proof yet that Saddam did possess materials for the making of weapons of mass destruction. In addition to the chemicals, U.S. troops found weapons stacked to the ceiling, including rocket-propelled grenades, mortars and AK-47s.

On Tuesday, April 8, Task Force Tarawa, a collection of U.S. Marine units, entered the town of Amara, located about 30 miles from the Iranian border. They had expected stiff resistance from the Iraqi 10th Armored Division, which had been bypassed by coalition ground troops during the opening days of war. But instead of a great battle, the Marines faced only token resistance, encircling the town and firing only two shots.

The Iraqi soldiers defending the town had apparently fled, abandoning their vehicles and disappearing into the countryside. "I just think they saw us coming and ran," shrugged Col. Richard Mills, commander of the 24th Marine Expeditionary Unit.

Added Lt. Col. Glenn Starnes: "The locals around there (said) they stacked their weapons, parked their vehicles and walked away. Right now, there is no enemy that we know of."

This was further proof of the sorry state of the Iraqi military as the war entered its 21st day. Faced with ever-growing American firepower, more and more Iraqi militiamen were calling it quits and going home. And no wonder: With U.S. forces steadily encroaching into Baghdad, it was obvious that Saddam's regime was gone.

The end of the war was all but official the next

day, when U.S. troops rolled into the heart of Baghdad to the cheers of hundreds of ecstatically happy citizens. Saddam's government was officially dissolved, the man himself missing and presumed dead. Newspapers around the world screamed the headline "Baghdad Falls!"

U.S. soldiers were mobbed by laughing Iraqis, many of whom couldn't wait to hug and kiss their liberators. "This is a good day for the Iraqi people," said Secretary of Defense Rumsfeld after the Army's 3rd Infantry Division and the 1st Marine Expeditionary Force met in the center of the city.

As news of the Americans' arrival spread through Baghdad, residents took to the streets in celebration. Many displayed their overwhelming rage at Saddam by angrily defacing images of the fallen dictator, tearing down posters bearing his picture and toppling statues. Some stopped in the middle of the street and began sobbing hysterically at the realization that the Saddam regime had finally been destroyed.

However, the war was not over. Though American forces had entered Baghdad and were there to stay, troops continued to meet pockets of resistance. Gunfire was exchanged at various locations as dedicated Fedayeen Saddam militia members took potshots at American forces.

The fighting continued for several more days as American forces raced to secure the city.

In the days following the liberation of Baghdad, many Iraqis looted stores and government buildings, carting off anything they could carry, no matter how impractical. Saddam's presidential palaces were especially popular targets and camera crews captured numerous images of Iraqi men and women in dirty, tattered clothing taking expensive furniture, paintings, kitchenware — even floral arrangements. "Saddam used my money to pay for these things," one man told journalists as he picked over what remained in one presidential palace. "It belongs to me."

Soldiers, more concerned with hunting down remaining enemy forces than with guarding storefronts, could only stand by as the looting increased. One of the few facilities that did receive military protection was Baghdad's largest hospital, which had been overwhelmed in recent days by a flood of sick and injured civilians. Smaller hospitals and clinics in the capital's surrounding suburbs weren't so lucky — looters picked them clean, right down to wall fixtures, within hours of the city's collapse.

Equally tragic was the loss of tens of thousands of priceless antiquities from the National Museum of Iraq, which housed one of the largest and most important collections of Middle Eastern artifacts in the world. Though relatively undamaged during the war, the museum was targeted by looters just days after American forces rolled into the city. The museum's curators did their best to protect the treasures, but their pleas didn't stop the rampaging mobs.

Among the items taken were a solid gold harp from the Sumerian era; a sculptured head of a woman from Uruk, one of the great Sumerian cities, and a collection of 4,000-year-old gold Sumerian necklaces, bracelets and earrings.

▬▬▬▬▬▬▬▬▬

The fall of Baghdad demonstrated that Saddam was no military genius. In fact, many military analysts believe that the dictator and his cronies had been victims of their regime's own propaganda, unaware until the final few hours of just how badly the war had gone for them.

"There is intelligence that indicated they didn't fully appreciate the mess they were in," a U.S. intelligence officer said. "Part of the problem is they believe their own spin."

Indeed, the Iraqi Ministry of Information had spread a wealth of lies to the Iraqi people throughout the entire war. Everything that happened was viewed through rose-colored glasses. Iraqi losses were never reported and every government-controlled newscast reported glowingly of Iraqi victories that never occurred. Toward the end, battle instructions were being sent to military divisions that no longer existed and many Iraqis had no idea that the Americans were at their gates until they actually saw tanks and other vehicles driving through the middle of town.

It's likely that even Saddam was left grossly uninformed by his own people, experts said. "Nobody wants to tell Saddam and senior leaders bad news, so lots of times they don't," the U.S. intelligence official explained. "They tend to believe things are going better than they are and before you know it, coalition forces are up close and personal."

In the wake of the American liberation of Baghdad, rumors spread rapidly regarding Saddam's fate: He was hiding in the Russian Embassy, desperately trying to arrange asylum. He and his family had fled across the border into Syria. He was hiding in his hometown of Tikrit. He was dead and remaining government officials had simply melted into the populace.

In truth, no one really knew what had befallen the deposed dictator in the days following the invasion of Baghdad. Most U.S. officials believed that he was dead, but there was no way of proving that. And without absolute proof from a reliable source, the possibility remained that he was alive — somewhere.

Meanwhile, reminders of the savagery of Saddam's regime were being found by British and

American forces as they captured key cities and towns throughout Iraq. Particularly stomach-churning were the torture chambers, many of them located in police stations and other government buildings. One such house of horror was uncovered in Nasiriyah, where a Marine patrol entered a building it thought was a police substation, only to find wooden stocks, an electric chair and other tools of torture amid reams of surveillance documents. "It (looked) a bit too much like Nazi Germany to me," said Capt. Pete McAleer, commander of the Echo Company of the 15th Marine Expeditionary Unit, which discovered the small compound.

At a prison in Basra, Iraqis showed journalists the white stone jail where for decades Saddam's secret police tortured inmates with beatings, electric shocks and chemical baths. Similar facilities were found in cities throughout the country — evidence of the cruelty the Saddam regime used to keep the Iraqi people in line. In many liberated towns, residents destroyed police and government buildings in acts of bitter defiance against the evil monsters who had committed such horrific acts against them.

On Thursday, April 10, Iraqi forces gave up the northern strongholds of Kirkuk and Mosul to a combination of coalition and Kurdish fighters as they swept toward Saddam's ancestral hometown of Tikrit in what was anticipated to be the final action of the war.

In both cities, resistance was practically nonexistent as Iraqi forces simply put down their weapons and went home. As soon as U.S. troops arrived, citizens took to the streets to greet their liberators and tear down all reminders of the former regime. By mid-day, looters began ransacking the cities, pillaging stores, banks and government buildings unchecked due to the temporary power vacuum that left the municipalities without a police force.

U.S. forces reported seeing numerous Iraqi soldiers, many still in uniform, walking along roads outside Kirkuk and Mosul. However, they were left alone because they were not carrying weapons. In many cases, the soldiers waved to passing American troops and a few even shouted, "Hurray America and Britain!"

Tikrit was an important coalition target — and one not likely to fall easily. As the hometown of Saddam Hussein, it held special importance to his faithful supporters, and American forces, who were then just 60 miles away, anticipated a fierce battle with remaining Republican Guard forces and other Saddam loyalists readying for a bloody showdown.

"They are the last significant formations on the battlefield that we're aware of," said Maj. Gen. McChrystal. "We are prepared to be very, very wary of what they might have and prepared for a big fight."

Meanwhile, chaos continued in Baghdad and other cities as American forces struggled to maintain control amid widespread looting, revenge attacks and sporadic battles with remaining Iraqi fighters. Baghdad looked like the Wild West as fierce firefights broke out between U.S. soldiers and Saddam loyalists near a mosque, a presidential palace and other locations. One Marine died and dozens were wounded in the fighting and four others were seriously injured when a suicide bomber walked up to a military checkpoint near the Palestine Hotel and detonated explosives attached to his body.

By Thursday night, tremendous fires raged in downtown Baghdad as looters torched government buildings and stores after stealing anything that could be carried away. U.S. officials promised the Iraqis that help was on its way, adding that it would take a little time to convert a military force into a temporary police force. "We do feel an obligation to assist in providing security," said Secretary of Defense Rumsfeld.

There was evidence of post-Saddam reform, however. In the western Iraq town of Rubah, villagers greeted coalition forces with open arms, begging them to stay to ward off the "death squads." The town later appointed a new mayor and installed a new government to replace Saddam's despised Baath Party.

By Friday, April 11, the battle plan for Tikrit was taking shape. U.S. intelligence reported that what was left of the Republican Guard's Adnan Division and other fighters — many of them mercenaries from neighboring Arab nations — was regrouping within the city. The enemy force appeared formidable, but U.S. military officials noted that it had been severely weakened by weeks of U.S. airstrikes and probably was not up to a protracted battle. Nonetheless, coalition forces weren't taking any chances, advancing cautiously and planning for any possibility.

The situation appeared a little better on the western front as Iraqi forces in the fiercely defended town of Al Qa'im, located near the Syrian border, appeared close to surrendering to American and British forces. "The fighting in Al Qa'im will be drawing to a close here shortly," assured Gen. Richard Myers, chairman of the Joint Chiefs of Staff.

Al Qa'im had strategic importance because facilities in the town had been used to extract a uranium derivative used in Saddam's nuclear program. Special teams searched the region for evidence of banned materials, Gen. Myers added.

In an effort to aid the search for Saddam and his inner circle, the U.S. Central Command gave troops decks of cards bearing the photos of the 52 most wanted individuals — with Saddam as the ace of spades. The cards were issued to give soldiers something to play with during down time, but also to help them identify high-ranking Iraqi officials who might try to sneak out of the country, a Pentagon spokesman said.

The U.S.-led coalition scored a tremendous coup Saturday, April 12, when Saddam's top science advisor, Lt. Gen. Amer al-Saadi surrendered to American forces in Baghdad. Al-Saadi, 64, was widely believed to be the mastermind behind Iraq's chemical weapons program, and was the chief liaison between the government and U.S. weapons inspectors. "He's a big fish," said a Marine intelligence officer. "A really big fish."

Added former U.N. chief nuclear weapons inspector David Kay: "(Al-Saadi) was at or near the center of (Iraq's) weapons programs from the 1980s on. If he talks, he could have a lot to say."

But as he was taken into custody, al-Saadi insisted again that Iraq no longer had weapons of mass destruction. Nor, he said, did he know the whereabouts of Saddam — or even if he was still alive.

Also on Saturday, U.S. officials announced that Iraqi police would patrol with Marines in Baghdad to help control looting and other problems. A total of 1,200 police and judicial officers were sent to help the U.S. military.

"Anyone who carries a weapon or fires a weapon, we will fire at," warned Iraqi police Col. Mohammed Zaki.

In Washington, Congress sent President Bush a nearly $80 billion emergency spending bill as partial payment for the cost of the war in Iraq and the nation's reconstruction. The package covered the first 30 days of combat in Iraq and also included funds for foreign aid, domestic security and the ailing airline industry.

"(This money) will help win the war and secure enduring freedom and democracy for the Iraqi people," said President Bush.

On Sunday, Marines heading toward Tikrit recovered seven American prisoners of war near the town of Samarra. The servicemen had been held captive for three weeks, but appeared to be in relatively good health. Five of the seven were members of the 507th Maintenance Company, the same unit to which Pvt. Jessica Lynch belonged.

Published reports said that a light armored detachment of Marines rescued the captured soldiers in a private residence after being notified of their location by local Iraqis. The POWs were rushed by helicopter to a base south of Baghdad, where they later boarded a plane to Kuwait so they could be checked out by Army doctors. "All of us feel a sense of relief," said Navy Lt. Mark Kitchens, a spokesman for U.S. Central Command in Qatar. "It is a great day."

Meanwhile, thousands of Marines approached Tikrit from the south, using helicopter gunships to destroy a column of Iraqi tanks. The Marines set up a perimeter around the town and sent in probes to determine the strength of the enemy. They were met by small-arms fire and the occasional rocket-propelled grenade, but the tremendous battle everyone had anticipated failed to materialize. Many residents said members of the Iraqi opposition had fled before the Marines arrived.

Nonetheless, U.S. forces played it safe. Despite the minimal resistance, they did not immediately enter the town. Instead, they massed for a huge invasion on three sides — a plan designed to overwhelm enemy forces through superior firepower. The next day, 3,000 Marines stormed into the heart of Tikrit, easily defeating the last of the hardcore resistance. Within hours, the city was almost fully in coalition hands — all that remained was a little mopping up.

In Baghdad, the city was divided into sections and Marine officers named unofficial "mayors" in an effort to quell the chaos that had overwhelmed the city since its capture by U.S. forces. The Marines were assigned to maintain law and order, collect weapons from civilians, stop looting and — perhaps most important — reassure residents that the war was quickly winding down and that the reconstruction process was in progress. Some of the units had interpreters, but most had to rely on English-speaking Iraqis to interpret during question-and-answer sessions.

On Monday, April 14, the Pentagon declared the end to significant fighting in Iraq. "The major combat operations are over," announced Maj. Gen. McChrystal — beautiful words to the anxious loved ones of American and British soldiers serving in Iraq.

Less than a month after coalition forces swept into the country, the primary mission of the war was complete. The people of Iraq were free and America and the world were safe. Saddam and his bloody regime had been eliminated, their tyranny forever a thing of the past.

The next job — the most important job — was

helping the beleaguered nation recover and rebuild. It was a daunting task, but the United States and the rest of the world were eager to help. No longer under Saddam's iron-fisted control, Iraq was ready to once again become an important, contributing member of the international community.

CHAPTER SEVEN

REBUILDING IRAQ

After nearly three decades of tyranny and terror, the people of Iraq now know the sweet taste of liberty.

But getting rid of Saddam was the easy part in the liberation of this ancient nation. More difficult will be its reconstruction, a massive undertaking that will take years (perhaps decades), billions of dollars and the cooperation of the entire world.

The challenge of rebuilding post-war Iraq was under discussion by the Bush administration long before the invasion began. The president knew that once Saddam was removed, the United States would have to move quickly to keep the peace and fill the leadership void. As a result, months were spent devising a transition plan that would give the nation back to its people as smoothly as possible.

The watchword always was liberation — never occupation. President George Bush did not want Iraq to become dependent on the United States or any other nation, as had happened through peacekeeping efforts in other parts of the world, such as Kosovo. The goal was to restore Iraq to what it had been before the rule of Saddam's ruthless regime: a flourishing, self-sufficient country that could take care of itself and its people.

The solution would have been much easier had Saddam simply chosen exile and left the country peacefully. There would have been less of a need to rebuild, allowing greater focus on the establishment of a democratic government and the reintroduction of Iraq as a viable, contributing member of the international community.

Of course Saddam didn't leave peacefully. Instead, he forced coalition forces to storm the country and take its major cities by force in order to dismantle his horrific regime. Strong resistance by Saddam's more fanatical supporters required American and British soldiers to use tanks, bombs and other devastating weapons to achieve their goal. The result, unfortunately, was a tremendous amount of damage to many of Iraq's major metropolitan areas.

Iraq's infrastructure quickly disintegrated as the war progressed. Food and clean water became scarce in many parts of the country, resulting in a nationwide humanitarian nightmare. Hospitals, many of them without running water or electricity, were overrun with civilian casualties — the war's most innocent victims. Coalition forces did what they could to help the innocents, but the chaos around them made the job extraordinarily difficult. On any given day, soldiers could find themselves in a vicious firefight with Republican Guard or Fedayeen Saddam forces, or in the role of providing much-needed medical care to injured locals and surrendering Iraqi conscripts.

When coalition forces finally took Baghdad, the idea of reconstruction seemed almost overwhelming. People were starving. Looters ran rampant because there were no police to stop them. Essential social services were all but nonexistent. The structural damage was devastating. And, most importantly, Iraq was a nation without an official leader.

President Bush assured the world during the early days of the war that the United States would work closely with the international community to rebuild Iraq after Saddam had been eliminated. He also vowed to "quickly seek new Security Council resolutions to encourage broad participation in helping the Iraqi people build a free Iraq."

But there was no question that the United States would lead the nation's rebirth. The president still had a bad taste in his mouth from the U.N. Security Council's unwillingness to approve force against Saddam when the dictator refused to disarm and he wasn't about to let the international body call the shots after the war was over. President Bush saw the United Nations' role as primarily humanitarian and advisory rather than rebuilding, a position that angered many world leaders, including the president's closest ally, British Prime Minister Tony Blair.

Certainly one of the biggest challenges in the reconstruction of Iraq will be getting the nation's religious and cultural factions to work peacefully together for the good of the nation. Ethnic tension is constantly simmering in Iraq, sparking fear among its neighbors that political unrest could lead to ongoing civil war, as has happened in Afghanistan. In that desert nation, also freed by American-led military action, a strong and continuous American presence has been required to maintain political stability.

"We feel the Americans will do the job militarily," a senior leader of one of Iraq's Arab neighbors was quoted as saying. "They're also talking about preserving the sovereignty, integrity and unity of

Iraq. The Arab countries and Iran also want this, but we're all worried that it won't happen. We're worried that the outcome will be civil war."

This concern — that the United States is taking on a job it will have to fight mightily to accomplish — is understandable. America has a checkered record when it comes to rebuilding nations. Japan and Germany were successfully rebuilt with U.S. assistance following World War II and today are healthy world powers. But there's a big difference between those nations and Iraq. Post-war Japan and Germany were well-educated, industrial nations with strong interim governments that worked closely with the United States and its allies. By comparison, the people of Iraq are not nearly as literate and aside from oil production the nation is not a major industrial power. Iraq is also strongly divided along religious lines, which could prove extremely problematic in choosing a leader. Similar problems were seen in Afghanistan.

The very first step toward the successful reconstruction of Iraq was — and will be — reassuring the people that coalition forces are their friends. Television coverage of the fall of Baghdad showed throngs of Iraqis greeting American soldiers with hugs and accolades, but there were many more throughout the country who viewed the troops with a strong sense of trepidation. It was, after all,

American bombs that had destroyed parts of their villages and cities, so a level of anxiety was to be expected.

To demonstrate the helpful intentions of American liberation forces, civil affairs officers quickly dispatched select troops to towns and cities to win Iraqi hearts and minds. Their job was to meet with community and religious leaders, assess structural damage and take the first steps toward fixing any war-related problems. The troops carried "rapid assessment" forms to evaluate and chart damage to homes and neighborhoods, and determine whether humanitarian aid was required. The troops were also to ensure that basic services such as water and sanitation systems were functioning.

"(The troops) can get a good information picture," explained Maj. Charles Brown, a civil affairs officer attached to the Army's 82nd Airborne Division. "They're going to try to be that interface between civilians and humanitarian assistance agencies such as the World Health Organization."

The effort is more than humanitarian — it's designed to win the complete support of the Iraqi people, a necessity if the American-led reconstruction effort is going to work. Such a move was extremely successful in Afghanistan, where villagers treated well by civil affair officers happily identified enemy soldiers and helped American troops locate caches of enemy weapons. It's hoped the program will be equally successful in Iraq.

———

The physical reconstruction of Iraq was scheduled to begin the moment hostilities officially ended and the last of Saddam's supporters had been rounded up. During the early days of the war, the Bush administration unveiled its reconstruction blueprint, which included allocating contracts — many worth hundreds of millions of dollars — to qualified American companies whose jobs it will be to repair just about everything damaged during the war or by Saddam's regime. The ongoing program will be overseen by the U.S. Agency for International Development.

An undertaking of this scale has not been seen since the Marshall Plan — America's reconstruction of Europe following World War II, said AID Administrator Andrew S. Natsios. Contractors will be called upon to repair Iraq's roads, hospitals, schools, airports, power plants and sewage systems, as well as assist in the creation of local governments and oversee the general health and welfare of the nation's 23 million people.

However, not all reconstruction contracts will be handled by AID. Contracts for the repair and running of Iraq's massive oil fields, for example, will be issued by the Pentagon, as will contracts pertaining to the reform of the Iraqi army and police — agencies previously rife with corruption and abuse.

In addition to rebuilding Iraq physically, the Bush administration plans to act quickly but carefully in establishing a viable government. As a replacement for Saddam, retired U.S. Army Lt. Gen. Jay Garner has been tapped to become the nation's chief interim civil administrator. It will be his responsibility to staff interim Iraqi government ministries with Iraqi bureaucrats uncorrupted by the Saddam regime or the Baath Party. It's hoped that many positions will be filled with prominent Iraqis who fled the country in the wake of Saddam and who desperately want to help rebuild their homeland.

Very early in the war, about 40 exiled Iraqi lawyers and judges met in Washington for legal training that would allow them to take part in temporary courts when the conflict ended. The two-week course was taught by U.S. Justice Department officials and outside experts in international law, war crimes and American-based judicial systems. "They want to introduce the Iraqis to the Anglo-Saxon legal system," explained one London-based Iraqi exile who was invited to attend.

Both the State Department and the Pentagon have actively recruited Iraqi exiles to assist the transition in post-war Iraq. The State Department's Future of Iraq Program has recruited more than 240 free Iraqis, as the exiles are called, to serve in 16 working groups. These groups deal with such important topics as defense policy, public health and national security. Because of the nature of the work, many of the recruited Iraqis hold advanced education degrees in a wide variety of subjects.

The Pentagon has recruited more than 100 free Iraqis for three- to six-month periods to help run provisional governments or work in various government ministries in Baghdad.

"The reason we're bringing them in is because they have lived in a democratic country. They understand the democratic process," a senior Pentagon official explained. "(Iraqi exiles) will help us facilitate making (specific ministries) more efficient."

Who ultimately will govern Iraq when the interim government leaves has been a matter of much debate in the United States and abroad. One of the front runners is Ahmed Chalabi, head of the Iraqi National Congress, a London-based Iraqi exile organization. Chalabi, who's very well-known within Washington's inner circles, helped convince many in the Bush administration that Saddam was a serious threat in need of elimination and has lobbied officials hard for a prominent position in post-Saddam Iraq — preferably the job of chief executive.

Some of the more conservative members of the Bush administration would like to see Chalabi in charge because he's a reformist and very pro-American. They also would like to see members of the Iraqi National Congress in key roles within the interim government. However, many officials within the State Department are reluctant to do so because Chalabi hasn't been in Iraq for decades and is something of an unknown to his countrymen.

A quick transition isn't as important as ensuring Iraq's international legitimacy, say some State Department officials. Many within the department would prefer to wait until a proposed post-war conference in Baghdad that would bring together leaders from all ethnic factions to create a well-rounded, inclusive and respected government.

All of these efforts, of course, are just the first building blocks in the massive reconstruction of a nation devastated by a corrupt regime and then by the war to remove that regime. In the inevitable chaos that resulted during the liberation of Iraq, the United States had an obligation to guarantee a smooth transition from dictatorship to democracy — an obligation it has worked mightily to meet.

Throughout it all, the message from President Bush has been clear: We and our allies are here to help Iraq, not conquer it. And the people have listened, ecstatically embracing their liberators as they look toward a future bright with promise.

APPENDICES

TIMELINE: THE LIFE OF

SADDAM HUSSEIN

Violence and bloodshed have always followed Saddam Hussein, as illustrated by this timeline of his personal life and political career:

1937: Saddam is born in the small village of al-Awja, located in the Tikrit region in northwest Iraq.

1947: Saddam is sent to live with his uncle in Baghdad because his mother and step-father can no longer care for him.

1957: Saddam becomes involved in the Arab nationalist movement and joins the Baath Party.

1958: Saddam is involved in the assassination of a prominent member of the Iraqi Communist Party. He is quickly arrested and spends six months in prison.

1959: The Baath Party recruits Saddam to help assassinate Iraqi leader Abd al-Karim Qassem, who is despised for his Communist sympathies. Qassem is wounded but not killed in the attack. Hussein is also wounded, taking a bullet to the leg. He flees to Syria dressed as a woman, then moves on to Egypt where he continues his education.

1960: Saddam is tried in absentia for the attempted assassination of Abd al-Karim Qassem and sentenced to death.

1963: The Baath Party briefly attains power by overthrowing Qassem's government. Saddam returns to Iraq to study law. The Baath Party loses power in a coup.

1964: Saddam is arrested and sent to prison. While behind bars, he is elected a leader of the Baath Party.

1965: The Baath Party returns as a formidable political force, with Ahmed Hassan al-Bakr as its secretary general.

1966: Saddam, still imprisoned, is made al-Bakr's deputy.

1967: Saddam escapes from prison.

1968: Saddam helps organize a bloodless coup that returns the Baath Party to power in Iraq. Al-Bakr is made president and Saddam is appointed acting deputy chairman of the Revolutionary Command Council (RCC), one of the government's most influential decision-making groups. In July, Saddam leads a purge of high-ranking individuals from the previous government.

1969: Saddam becomes a leading force within the Baath Party and is confirmed as deputy chairman of the RCC. During this period he begins assisting the Kurds in their quest for autonomy. The relationship will eventually sour, leading to years of unrest and bloodshed.

1970: Saddam is placed in charge of a covert surveillance organization established by the ruling Baath Party. He becomes a member of the ruling triumvirate, which includes al-Bakr and General Adnan Khayr Allah Talfah – Saddam's brother-in-law.

1971: Saddam receives his law degree from the University of Baghdad.

1972: Saddam oversees the nationalization of Iraq's vital oil industry.

1975: Following a year of conflict with Kurdish separatists, Saddam weakens their support base by settling a long-standing dispute with Iran over ownership of the Shatt al Arab – the point at which the Tigris and Euphrates rivers meet. No longer aided by Iran, the Kurdish dissidents are forced to give up the fight. Thousands of Kurds are relocated and all Kurdish villages along the Iran-Iraq border are destroyed.

1976: Saddam introduces a popular state-sponsored

modernization program aimed at improving education and health care.

1977: Saddam assumes full control of the government when al-Bakr becomes too ill to govern.

1978: Saddam expels Shiite cleric Ayatollah Sayyid Khomeini, who later becomes head of Iran following an Islamic revolution that ousts the Shah.

1979: Saddam is appointed president of Iraq when al-Bakr officially steps down. Saddam's power is consolidated further when he also is made secretary-general of the Baath Party Regional Command, chairman of the RCC and commander-in-chief of Iraq's armed forces. Within days of his presidential appointment, Saddam initiates a bloody purge of anyone he considers a threat within the government and the military.

1980: Iraqi Shiites, inspired by the success of their Iranian brothers, target high-ranking Iraqi cabinet members in an attempt to overthrow the government. Saddam responds with an iron fist, ordering the immediate deportation of thousands of Iranian-born Shiites and the swift execution of the Shiite opposition leader.

Later in the year, Saddam provokes a war with Iran by canceling the 1975 agreement and sending troops across the border.

1982: With the war going badly, Saddam attempts to

negotiate a cease-fire with Iran. The effort fails and Iranian forces continue their offensive, crossing the Shatt al Arab and, aided by the Kurds, taking several mountain passes in the north.

Later, the Saddam regime executes thousands of Iranian prisoners of war and Kurdish civilians, proving yet again its total disregard for human life.

1984: Following years of political animosity, diplomatic relations between the United States and Iraq are restored, resulting in much-needed aid. For a brief period, Saddam poses as a friend of the United States.

1988: A cease-fire with Iran is finally declared. However, the war has ravaged both nations with an estimated 75,000 Iraqis killed and another 250,000 wounded. The cost of the physical damage inflicted on Iraq is estimated in the tens of billions of dollars.

Saddam takes revenge on the Kurds who aided Iran by attacking their settlements with chemical weapons, killing thousands. In addition, an estimated 4,000 Kurdish villages are completely destroyed and innumerable Kurds are forcibly deported. The atrocities do little to help the nation's already shaky relationship with the United States.

1990: Just two years after the end of the devastating Iran-Iraq war, Saddam invades neighboring Kuwait under the pretext that Kuwait has always belonged to Iraq. The United Nations quickly imposes sanctions against Iraq.

1991: When Saddam ignores a U.N. resolution demanding Iraq's immediate withdrawal from Kuwait, a U.S.-led coalition picks up the gauntlet. The six-week war, known as Operation Desert Storm, quickly sends the Iraqis fleeing. Coalition forces chase Saddam's rag-tag army to just outside Baghdad.

Shortly after agreeing to a cease-fire, Saddam again turns his tyranny against the Kurds in the north and the Shiite Arabs in the south. In both regions, entire villages are destroyed and thousands of villagers are sent fleeing.

1992: International leaders demand that Saddam destroy his weapons of mass destruction under the watchful eye of U.N. weapons inspectors. Not surprisingly, Saddam grants inspectors only limited access.

1994: Saddam is appointed prime minister of Iraq. Later in the year, he attempts to bully his way around international trade sanctions by once again amassing troops at the Kuwaiti border. He quickly backs down when threatened with retaliation by international coalition forces.

1995: A national referendum grants Saddam another seven-year term as president of Iraq.

1997: Saddam orders that all Kurds be forcibly removed from the Kirkuk region north of Baghdad. Ethnic Arabs resettle the area.

1998: Angered by continued U.S. participation,

Saddam stops cooperating with U.N. weapons inspectors. The inspectors leave the country in December, just before the United States and Great Britain begin an extended bombing campaign against suspected Iraqi weapons facilities.

2000: The International Commission of the Red Cross and other agencies report that Saddam's use of "oil for food" money to fund his exorbitant lifestyle and to pay off supporters has plunged Iraq into a humanitarian crisis that threatens the health and lives of millions of Iraqis – particularly the nation's children. Saddam is thought to have squandered more than $2 billion just on presidential palaces, an indication that his own luxury was far more important to him than the well-being of his people.

2002: President George W. Bush designates Iraq a member of the "axis of evil" (along with Iran and North Korea) following terrorist attacks on the World Trade Center and the Pentagon. The stage is set for the United States and its allies to take down one of the world's most ruthless dictators.

2003: Coalition forces, led by the United States and Great Britain, launch a massive military campaign to end the blood-soaked regime of Saddam Hussein and bring freedom and democracy to an impoverished Iraq.

TIMELINE: A BRIEF

HISTORY OF IRAQ

F ew nations on Earth are as rich in history and heritage as Iraq. Located on a large section of the region once known as Mesopotamia, it is commonly regarded as the cradle of civilization. Following is a timeline of troubled region's development:

5000 BC: First human settlements established.

3000 BC: Sumerians construct cities in lower Mesopotamia.

1900 BC: Amorite Empire begins.

1600 BC: Hittite Empire begins.

1500 BC: Kassite Empire is founded in central Mesopotamia.

1200 BC: Assyrian Empire begins.

612 BC: Chaldean Empire begins.

539-331 BC: Persian Empire controls Mesopotamia.

331-170 BC: Greek/Macedonian Empire, established by Alexander the Great, controls Mesopotamia.

126 BC: Parthian Empire takes over.

227 AD: Sassanid Empire controls Mesopotamia.

638-1100: Arab Empire controls the region. Often called the Golden Age of Baghdad.

1258-1355: Mongols invade Mesopotamia. Baghdad is sacked.

1355-1400: Jalayirids control the region.

1401-1405: Tamerlane invades Mesopotamia. Baghdad is sacked again.

1500-1722: Savafid Empire rules Mesopotamia.

1534-1918: The Age of the Ottoman Empire. The provinces of Baghdad, Basra and Mosul are established and will later form modern Iraq.

1914: With World War I in full swing, Britain invades Mesopotamia to protect interests in Iran and India.

1919: At the Paris Peace Conference, the state of Iraq is created and placed under British control.

1921: Faisal I is made King of Iraq, though the nation remains under British rule.

1932: Iraq gains its independence and is admitted into the League of Nations.

1934: Iraq begins exporting oil.

1941: Great Britain invades Iraq a second time and establishes a pro-British government in Baghdad.

1945: Iraq is admitted to the United Nations and is a founding member of the Arab League.

1948-49: The Israel War of Independence. Iraq participates in attacks on the fledgling state.

1954: President Dwight Eisenhower approves military aid to Iraq in an effort to protect American oil interests in the region. This severely weakens British influence.

1958: The Arab Union is formed between Iraq and Jordan. Also that year, Gen. Abdul Karim Qassem heads a coup that successfully overthrows the Hashemite monarchy.

1959: Iraq claims sovereignty over Kuwait and additional territory along the Shatt al Arab waterway, which leads to the Persian Gulf.

1960: Iraq threatens to invade Kuwait. A strong British military response prevents the invasion.

1963: A coup by the Baath Party overthrows the Republican government. Six months later, the Baath Party is also overthrown.

1968: A Baath Revolution establishes the party's control over Iraq.

1973: Iraq participates in the Six-Day War against Israel. The conflict eventually leads to a peace accord between Egypt and Israel, and re-establishes Iraq's leadership in pan-Arab affairs.

1979: Saddam Hussein becomes president of Iraq, replacing Hassan al-Bakr.

1980: The Iran-Iraq War begins.

1981: Israel bombs an Iraqi nuclear reactor.

1982: An Iraqi-announced cease-fire in the war is ignored by Iran, which pushes into Iraqi territory.

1983: Iranian forces attack northern Iraq.

1984: Iraq uses mustard gas against Iranian forces in central Iraq.

1986: Saddam again proposes a cease-fire. The Ayatollah Khomeini rejects it.

1987: Iraq accidentally strikes the *USS Stark* with a missile, killing 37 American sailors. Saddam apologizes.

1988: The Iran-Iraq War ends in a U.N.-imposed cease-fire. Also that year, Saddam authorizes the use of chemical weapons against Kurds living near Halabja. More than 5,000 Kurds die in the attack.

1990: Iraq invades Kuwait, leading to Operation Desert Shield – a military buildup in Saudi Arabia by coalition forces.

1991: American-led coalition forces chase Iraq out of Kuwait during Operation Desert Storm. Iraq launches Scud missiles into Israel and Saudi Arabia in an attempt to draw Israel into the conflict and destroy the U.S.-Arab Coalition. Later that year, a no-fly zone is established in northern Iraq to protect Kurdish settlers.

1992: A no-fly zone is established in southern Iraq.

1993: Saddam Hussein authorizes the assassination of former President George Bush while Bush is visiting Kuwait. The Clinton administration responds by lobbing cruise missiles at an Iraqi intelligence center in Baghdad.

1994: Iraq again threatens to invade Kuwait and positions forces at the border as a show of strength. American and British bombing raids force their withdrawal.

1998: Iraq evicts United Nations weapons inspectors.

2002: President George W. Bush calls Iraq a member of the "axis of evil," along with Iran and North Korea.

2003: American-led coalition forces invade Iraq. Their goal: Eliminate Saddam Hussein.

TIMELINE: TO WAR

Sept. 12, 2002: A year and a day after the terrorist attacks on the World Trade Center and the Pentagon, President George W. Bush announces his intent to get rid of Saddam Hussein, calling the dictator "a grave and gathering danger."

Sept. 13: Iraqi Deputy Prime Minister Tariq Aziz says President Bush's speech is "full of lies."

Sept. 16: Iraq attempts to placate the world by announcing that U.N. weapons inspectors can return without conditions.

Sept. 17: France, Russia, China and the Arab nations say Iraq's offer should be sufficient to hold off stronger action.

Sept. 18: President Bush calls Saddam's offer "a ploy."

Sept. 19: President Bush asks Congress for authorization to use all means that he determines necessary – including force – to defend the United States against the threat posed by Iraq. Saddam responds by saying Iraq has no weapons of mass destruction and that America's true goal is Iraqi oil.

Sept. 20: The White House unveils a strategic doctrine that endorses pre-emptive action against international threats.

Sept. 26: Secretary of Defense Donald Rumsfeld says evidence shows that al Qaeda terrorists were in Baghdad and that the terrorist network has asked Iraq for help in acquiring weapons of mass destruction.

Sept. 30: Iraq announces that it wants to restore diplomatic relations with Iran.

Oct. 1: Chief U.N. weapons inspector Hans Blix says that Iraq has agreed to terms for inspections, but that eight presidential sites are not included.

Oct. 7: President Bush calls on Congress to back him on Iraq, noting that the congressional resolution does not mean that military action is unavoidable.

Oct. 10: The House of Representatives approves a resolution authorizing President Bush to use force against Iraq if necessary. The vote is 296-133.

Oct. 11: By a vote of 77-23, the Senate also authorizes President Bush to use force against Iraq.

Oct. 21: Bush says he doesn't believe Saddam will fully disarm, but that if the dictator does meet all conditions it would mean "the regime has changed."

Oct. 26: An anti-war march in Washington draws nearly 100,000 protesters. It is the first of many worldwide.

Nov. 7: The U.N. Security Council unanimously passes a resolution demanding new weapons inspections in Iraq and sets a timetable for them. Iraq is given until Nov. 15 to accept the resolution.

Nov. 13: Iraq accepts the U.N. resolution.

Nov. 18: A U.N. advance team arrives in Iraq to conduct the first weapons inspections in nearly four years.

Nov. 21: NATO approves a resolution calling on Saddam to disarm but fails to mention military action if he refuses.

Nov. 27: U.N. weapons inspectors get to work.

Dec. 7: Iraq gives the U.N. a 12,000-page report detailing its programs for weapons of mass destruction. Saddam goes on television to apologize to the people of Kuwait for the 1990 invasion of their country.

Jan. 7, 2003: The Pentagon starts to establish a headquarters staff in Qatar. International opposition to a war begins to build.

Jan. 10: Secretary of Defense Rumsfeld signs an order authorizing the deployment of up to 130,000 troops to the Persian Gulf by March.

Jan. 13: U.N. weapons inspectors say they will need at least six months to complete their work in Iraq.

Jan. 14: President Bush condemns Iraq's noncompliance with weapons inspectors, noting that he is "sick and tired" of the nation's games.

Jan. 16: U.N. weapons inspectors find 11 artillery shells capable of holding chemical weapons.

Jan. 17: Secretary of Defense Rumsfeld suggests that Saddam go into exile, thus saving his nation from being ravaged yet again by war.

Jan. 20: Iraq agrees to let weapons scientists be interviewed within the country, but refuses to allow overflights by American spy planes.

Jan. 22: French and German leaders say they're opposed to military action in Iraq. NATO refuses to vote on providing military support to Turkey.

Jan. 26: Secretary of State Powell says he no longer has faith in U.N. weapons inspections and that time is "running out" for Saddam.

Jan. 27: Hans Blix tells the United Nations that Iraq has not displayed a "genuine acceptance" of international demands to disarm.

Jan. 28: During his State of the Union address, President Bush warns "if Saddam Hussein does not fully disarm ... we will lead a coalition to disarm him."

Jan. 29: The leaders of several nations, including Britain, the Czech Republic, Italy and Spain say they support President Bush's vow to disarm Saddam by force if necessary. However, 11 of the 15 U.N. Security Council members say they support continued inspections.

Feb. 4: Hans Blix says the Iraq war clock is at "five

minutes to midnight." Israeli and American troops test Patriot missile-interceptor batteries.

Feb. 5: During an address before the United Nations, Secretary of State Powell offers intercepted phone calls and satellite photos that he says prove Iraq is hiding its weapons of mass destruction program.

Feb. 13: President Bush chastises the United Nations, saying it must help the United States confront Saddam or risk becoming irrelevant. Secretary of State Powell tells Congress that the nation should prepare for "a fairly long-term commitment" in Iraq.

Feb. 17: NATO agrees to discuss how to defend Turkey in case of war. In addition, the first U-2 flight is sent over Iraq.

Feb. 20: Secretary of Defense Rumsfeld says enough troops are now in the Persian Gulf for a successful invasion.

Feb. 24: The United States, Britain and Spain introduce a U.N. resolution declaring Saddam in violation of orders to disarm.

Feb. 27: Iraq agrees "in principle" to destroy a banned missile system.

March 1: The Turkish parliament votes to ban U.S. troops from using Turkish military bases.

March 2: Iraq begins destroying its al-Samoud 2 missiles. Bahrain, Kuwait and the United Arab Emirates ask Saddam to step down for the benefit of his people.

March 7: Hans Blix delivers a report to the United Nations stating that weapons inspections will take months, not weeks.

March 12: Britain offers a compromise resolution outlining six specific disarmament steps Iraq would have to take to prevent war.

March 13: France rejects the British compromise.

March 16: President Bush, British Prime Minister Tony Blair and Spanish Prime Minister Jose Maria Aznar meet in the Azores to discuss the Iraq situation. President Bush says the U.N. is facing a "moment of truth."

March 17: In a televised address, President Bush tells Saddam he has 48 hours to leave Iraq or face war. The United Nations orders all personnel out of Iraq.

March 18: Saddam rejects President Bush's ultimatum.

March 19: President Bush authorizes war. In an effort to decapitate the Iraqi central command, U.S. forces launch cruise missiles at targets in Baghdad where senior Iraqi leaders are thought to be located.